Ivan, An... ...ach a world characterized by
ambiguity, contradiction, ...lexity/unknowability which is
simultaneously smaller, faster, flatter. Quintessential question.

[fa...
Ort... ...ot?

Is it Yves ... ...rything that is solid turns
into...)? ... ...you've made... this collaborative trans-local, networked (your words) thinking, seeing, constructing the intersections of human experience. Specializing in placeless-ness and ephemerality.

Visualizing, theorizing the invisible (Fuller said, "Architecture is in the end invisible," didn't he?)

The intangibility of the virtual as an escape? Or is it a reprieve from the day to day, the ordinary? Or is it the vast limitation of the material world with its constraints of gravity and such, (and all that is habitual)?

This scaffolding, neither here nor there (your practice), intent on liberating us of all these constraints, re-establishing the processes and patterns of boundlessness. All is open, fluid, mobile, fluctuating. A re-emergence, a reconfiguration of thought patterns articulated in the sixties? Yona (Friedman), Constance, Cedric (Price) and the Archigram boys, with the investment of Marinettian speed and acceleration.
[fast forward]
Ortlos. or not?

[FAST FORWARD]
ORTLOS. OR NOT?

lighthings, spiral skins, city at once, natural networks...attempts to reinvent, reconfigure, establish cultural relationships into new emergent behaviors. Peripatetic, nomadic (your thinking), with no interest in categorization, but in intersections, non-sequiturs. Celebrating visual overstimulation, the equivalency of photography, graphics, architecture, advertising, film.

X = X.

Thom Mayne

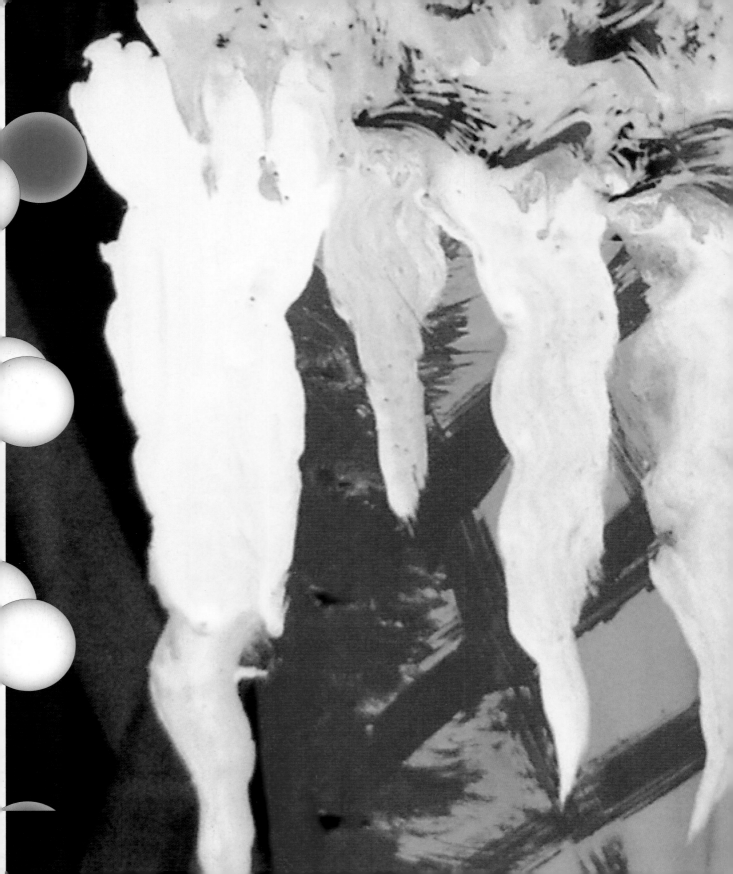

ortlos

.archi
tec-
.archite
ture of
ture of
the
the
net.work.

Hatje Cantz

Editors: Ivan Redi & Andrea Redi - ORTLOS architects.

Translations: A & A Peaston, Graz

Graphic design: David Carson Design

Foreword: Thom Mayne, Morphosis

Printing: Dr. Cantz'sche Druckerei, Ostfildern-Ruit

Published by
Hatje Cantz Verlag
Senefelderstrasse 12
73760 Ostfildern-Ruit
Germany
Tel. +49 711 4405-0
Fax +49 711 4405-220
www.hatjecantz.com

Hatje Cantz books are available internationally at selected bookstores and from the following distribution partners:

USA/North America - D.A.P., Distributed Art Publishers, New York, www.artbook.com
UK - Art Books International, London, sales@art-bks.com
Australia - Towerbooks, French Forest (Sydney), towerbks@zipworld.com.au
France - Interart, Paris, commercial@interart.fr
Belgium - Exhibitions International, Leuven, www.exhibitionsinternational.be
Switzerland - Scheidegger, Affoltern am Albis, scheidegger@ava.ch

For Asia, Japan, South America, and Africa, as well as for general questions, please contact Hatje Cantz directly at sales@hatjecantz.de, or visit our homepage www.hatjecantz.com for further information.

ISBN 3-7757-1652-1

Printed in Germany

Cover, illustration: David Carson Design

Frontispiece: Conceptual sketch for A.N.D.I. / ORTLOS architects

All graphics and photos courtesy of ORTLOS architects unless otherwise noted.

photo: david carson

ORTLOS is a virtual office (or platform)deal-
ing with architectural topics,urban planning issues and interface design in general.
Its members are experts from different
countries with different professions (architects,web designers,media theorists,net
artists and IT specialists).
The name (ORTLOS means "placeless "or
"space off "in German)describes the basic
working method:not being dependent on
a certain place to work,but rather located
in networks and anywhere where an Internet connection is provided.Furthermore,
thinking and designing in trans-local and
networked environments is crucial to the
concept of ORTLOS.
The users are well acquainted with their
localities and can deal (or not)with the
problems of the city they live in.As soon as
they have an internet connection,they can
work on projects in this "office that never
sleeps ".
The aim is to generate advanced instru-
ments for architectural and urban
design,a
sort of platform,a creative pool supported
with information and databases.
The two main topics of ORTLOS are experimental architecture and interface design
in
urban surroundings.

www.ortlos.com

ORTLOSorNOt?

ORTLOS NET

shivendu jauhari (IN)

martin frühwirth (AUT)

Katrin Knass (A)

bernd grabner (AUT)

djordje kitic (YU)

qing-feng chen(CN)

vincent cellier (F)

nebojsa dinic (YU)

markus möderl(AUT)

angelika sprinz (AUT)   peter holzmann (AUT)   kira kirsch(D)

sinisa ilic (BiH)

ORTLOS architects was founded in Graz in 2000 by Ivan Redi and Andrea Schröttner at the time that the two young architects were given the enormous opportunity to present their ideas and work at the world-famous architecture exhibition La Biennale di Venezia.
One September day in 1999 an e-mail arrived which read:"Dear Mr. Ortlos,we kindly invite you to participate at next year's architectural exhibition in Venice.The theme is 'Less Aesthetics,More Ethics '. Sincerely yours,Massimiliano Fuksas,Director ".After submitting some of their work to the on-line competition,together with their friend Martin Frühwirth,and reviewing it on the Internet,Mr.Fuksas gave them a great honor by inviting them.

The beginning was exemplary of **ORTLOS** 's commitment to the Internet and on-line working methods as well as their strong interest in expanding classical architectural tasks by simulating virtual environments to be applied to future realities,net,art,and the wide use of cutting-edge computer technologies.

The new generative processes and design strategies come from the independent field of open-source communities and go far beyond architectural dogmas,rigid academic institutions and "schools ".

Ivan Redi (1971) was born in Nis,Serbia,is an
Austrian citizen,and gained working experience at Morphosis,Santa Monica,USA,and he is also a licensed architect in Holland.He received his diploma from the Technical University in Graz,where Günther Domenig was his mentor.He also studied in Thom Mayne 's and Daniel Libeskind 's classes and is currently working on his PhD thesis:"New design methods in architecture ".He teaches at TU Graz.

Andrea Schröttner – Redi (1966) was born
in Graz,Austria.She received her diploma with distinction from the Technical University in Graz and won the Speer Urban Prize,as well as

numerous student competitions.She has tremendous building experience —especially in sustainable environments,and she is a licensed architect in Austria.
She is currently working on her PhD:"New Interfaces".She teaches at TU Graz.

_9

Designed and written by augmented and complementary partners,
ORTLOS:ARCHITECTURE OF THE NETWORKS documents projects from
2000 to 2003 as a culmination of the first phase in the development
of the ORTLOS p h e n o m e n a .

11:06:29   2-MAY-2001

22:54:39 18-AUG-2001

12:21:07   4-OCT-2001

11:18:10 27-MAR-2002

CyberDandy
ORTLOS
or NOT?

"If media is the answer, the question must be fucking stupid!"

4 o 'clock in the afternoon in Graz is a good time. The stress of the morning is over (getting up, making phone calls, writing faxes, checking the news groups and reading e-mails), so is the subsequent lunch break with espresso, and finally one can start to concentrate on work. Our friends in Los Angeles have just returned from surfing and are ready for the teleconference, in New York everything has long since been in full swing, and while in Belgrade the great heat wave is slowly passing, the Internet time of 625 in Bangalore suggests it is already time to store reports and files on the server before going out for a drink. The flood of information, images and sounds coming in adding to the workload, together with the possibility of being able to communicate and retrieve information any time, disturb the withdrawn and concentrated working situation of the lonely thinker sitting in front of the emptiness of a white sheet of paper.

The afternoon sun is squeezing through the gap between the sun shades of a café in the main square of Sienna in Tuscany, caressing a glass of Chianti on a round table before it is lifted by a hand. The table fills up quickly as the same hand immediately after unpacks a laptop, a palm pilot and mobile (adding to the ash tray, salt cellar and the menu). The laptop boots up, the palm pilot is synchronized, and the mobile turned in the direction of the infra-red interface. But suddenly the battery symbol starts flashing —it must be defective or empty; the synchronizing process has not been completed because the COM1 port is going crazy and the cracked Data Suite Software for the Nokia mobile doesn 't work because the infra-red interface only runs on COM1, thus making the reading and sending of e-mails impossible. That very moment the camera cuts abruptly to a shot of the Chianti glass, the picture fades out and the writing is dissolved, "If you have a deadline, you better stay offline ...". This was an excerpt from the latest anti-ortlos TV commercial, which will be broadcast this fall on every household.

Since most architects and artists are not skilled technicians, complex working processes often have to be carried out with proper technicians. The outcome of this translation of ideas can only be imagined. Everything appears as a collage or montage of thought fragments, pushed back and forth for a specific purpose. For somebody who is not in full command of the tool that he should be able to use day after day will have difficulty working on new concepts and ideas. But work and works of art are no longer the expression of a single individual as was still the case in Romanticism and classical Modernity. Neither, however, is it the expression of a collective as in the middle of the 20th century. Rather, it is the expression of a platform, a network of influences, continuously being reorganized by all participants. **Discursive forums and artistic practices that do not aim for any durability take the place of the individual work of a single artist or group of artists.** Their temporary nature creates the precondition for the inherent opportunity for constant change. This could be a model, in post-industrial societies, for how, as many people as possible can be led to participate in social processes.

13

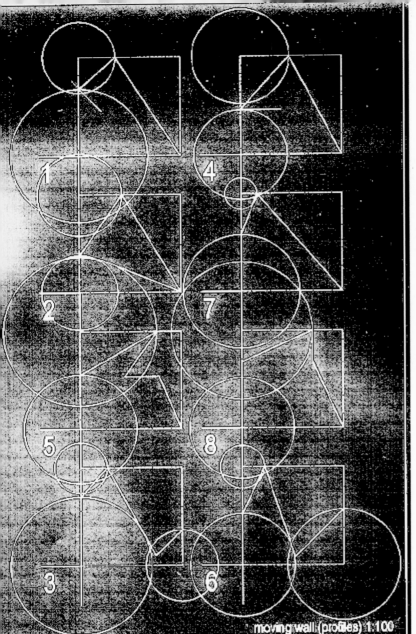

moving wall (profiles) 1:100

If architects only knew what they could possibly sell and distribute,
they would have long since got into e-business.The profession of architect is one that wishes to be seen as a service with-out,however,
wanting to give up the creative aspect.Our scenario:you set up a digital platform following the "open source "principle.This means,just
as with software,not something available for free down-load,but an
offer of a public code for further development.However,we should
not deduct a formal presentation from this,but envisage clearly
structured and documented algorithms of developmen-tal processes
that describe the various interfaces.By understanding the network
as space for communication,and not presentation,we believe that
the design of visual language is an important step where the visualization of space takes place through controlled simula-tion.Talking of
spacelessness or of the elimination of space merely obscures the fact
that it is not only that cyberspace creates new spaces,new property
and new kinds of power but that,in fact,these manifest in real space.
From a market strategy point of view,a lethal competi-tion is building
up between what is real and what is virtual.Non-places are arising
from the collapse of localities and bases in the process of globaliza-
tion,which is unprecedented in history.

The two main themes of **ORTLOS** are experimental architecture and interface design in urban sur-roundings.In our projects "Library of the information age ","Teleworking House in Kotor "and "City at once ",but also in our installation at the Biennale,we have made a theme of the interlinking of media theory via the information society in which we live and architecture,and especially the virtuality which we trust,in order to simulate and check the real worlds that we experience.Since architecture has an ethical problem with everything that is not static,and feels committed to its traditional role of giving shelter and thus to a culture of stasis,the challenge is to get rid of any idealized utopian ideological ideas.The first steps in this direction are above all improved communication on the part of the users and developers,and the generating of complex systems of parametrically process-like decisions.The starting point here would be a simple understanding for the environments that influence our lifestyle. The projects about and for the city,in contrast to urban building projects,have a different logic and develop their own existence.Our project "City at Once "starts a priori from the complexity of the ur-ban without being subject to predetermined deconstructivist methods.

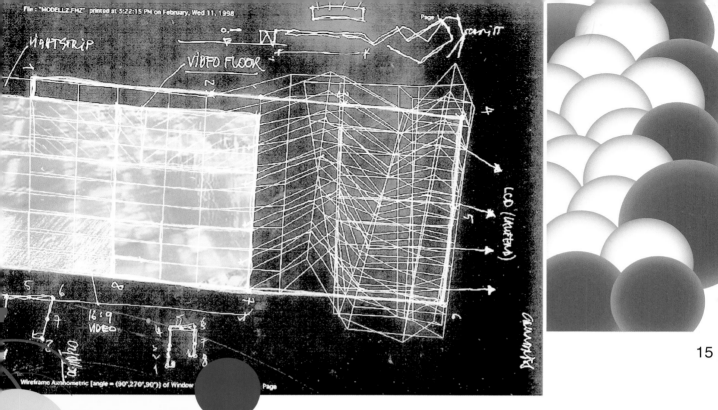

File: "MODELLZ.FMZ" printed at 5:22:15 PM on February, Wed 11, 1998

NIGHTSTRIP
VIDEO FLOOR
LCD (VERTICAL)
16:9 VIDEO

Wireframe Axonometric [angle = (90°,270°,90°)] of Window ... Page

A draft plan of the urban,however,can only be achieved by including time.The manifestation of the geometries shown in the plan is the result of the generative process.Form is dependant on time and the actors.Just like the dwellers in a city,the planners decide on their preferences on the basis of precise function and transport schemes.On the surface, they realize the possibilities from a mass of information,organization,experience and inspiration.An abstract set of rules steers this inductive process that is non-deterministic.It is only with the help of computer simulation technology that time can be depicted in the form of this concept.The flexible form of time is difficult to grasp for the untrained eye in conventional architectural drawings.Only when we include the time factor in our representation,we can make the flow of processes comprehensible.Of course,a result always fulfils the pragmatic requirements of function,but the appearance is dependent on time,the users and what there was to start with.The form fully emancipates itself without any claim to right or wrong,beautiful or ugly.These categories become superfluous.They unite in one single fluid mass of geometries.It would be ideal for ORTLOS projects to have everything on one single page,to spread everything on one and the same surface: real events,historical conditions,ideas,individuals,social groups and constellations.This one "hyper site "is not to be understood geometrically as a surface,but as an active,abstract matrix —AWSP (Active Work Server Pages)...as a kind of illustration of the relations between the various data systems.

The name **ORTLOS** can be basically seen as a statement about our working method:not space-bound,in networks and everywhere where there is an Internet connection.This is an important pre-condition because new working worlds and structures evolve in this way,and thus the whole process has a strong impact on work itself.The structures are adapted to the individual settings depending on the analysis of the situation (e.g.for Mexico City and Los Angeles different settings and preferences are required compared to New York or Tokyo,let alone small cities,such as Graz ...).Users are familiar with the local situation and know the problems "on site ".All they need is access to the internet,and they can work on projects in "an office that never sleeps ".The aim is to create a progressive instrument for architecture and urban planning tasks,a platform or creative pool supported by information data bases.

ORTLOS must be a kind of matrix,an infinite,constantly changeable field of the creative entries of those who shape it.From a certain size on,the constructs show the first signs of self-organization.

And so it has been with **ORTLOS** right from the beginning.It is a kind of virus that is spreading,and although in the background,it makes you gradually sink into a world whose laws correspond to a different logic …

When a closed and rational system of the computer network merges with the incoherent rhizomatous structure of urban space,numerous interfaces originate,some of them growing wild,and thus existing topologies acquire a new dimension.Spaceless.But spaceless is dimensionless.It means no organized memory and no central mechanism,defined solely by a circulation of conditions.ORTLOS is an instrument for the nomadic working methods.

Final remarks.

For whom is it intended ? What is the objective ? What is the reason for it ? These are unnecessary questions.Tabula Rasa is also wrong.You start from the middle,which does not represent an average value,but spaceless space,where things are accelerated

City at once
Los Angeles,
USA

MASTERPLAN -City at once

The working title could also be "THE PROJECT NOT YET DESIGNED" since we have gained extraordinary experiences working on this huge site 7 km long and 3 km wide. At the moment when city planning has almost become obsolete and we are faced with the indescribably complexity of the urban environment, the process becomes more important then one man 's decision. We use computers at every stage of design, or more accurately "research "; not only for "data processing " but for simulations of possibilities and behaviors of urban parameters. Taken as a reference, this project opens discussions on the inter-textual boundaries within all of our projects. Non-linearity, multi-dimensionality, acceleration, compression, multiple layers, poly-perspectives and multi-functionality are some of the key words. It also emphasizes interfaces, not realities. Interfacing doesn 't deal with negotiating between realities, but acts in a field of effects where the natural and the artificial can no longer be easily distinguished. It is a paradigm shift from viewing cities in formal terms to looking at them in dynamic ways. The familiar urban typologies of square, park, district, and so on are of less use or significance than are the infrastructures, network flows, ambiguous spaces, and other polymorphous conditions that constitute the contemporary metropolis.

Tula Ferrera

The Playa Vista is unique by virtue of its size,location and natural beauty.With 400 hectares,it is 30 percent larger than New York 's Central Park.Its location,which is within minutes of airport LAX and includes two freeways and the key Westside beach area,is one of the most desirable in south California.Two striking natural elements –the Pacific coastline and the Westchester and Playa del Rey Bluffs define the site 's character and beauty.

The first step in architectural organization and ordering of large human settlements is produced by texture rather than geometry.It is a matrix which demonstrates the hypothesis of urban generators or architectural systems in the city,and acts as catalysts for every kind of activity or function,independent of the form that they may take.The second definition can be a landscape as active surface a structuring of the conditions for new relationships and interactions among the things its supports. We developed a textural mapping method based on the superimposition of autonomous systems and combinations of computer-manipulated abstract pieces coming from outside of the site involving this area in international backgrounds,juxtaposition of 3-dimensional basic programmatic areas based on difference and cultural discontinuity,different building topologies and finally overlayed with topological particularities of the site ⁻marina,ocean front,bluffs,wetlands.

←←←←Tula   Ferrera

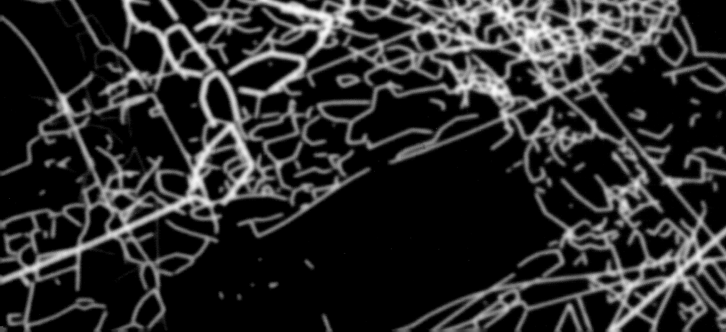

Those elements are now merged together,and are applied as a two-dimensional diagram to the site.In a search for the connection within the existing environment the given boundaries are not considered.The result is meant to be a programmable form (function +geometry). This plan is a departure point for the solution of architectural decisions according to programmatic parameters.The parameters are defining the geometry,which is based on editable meshes. The extension of the new marina,whose curved line path of basin is also connected with Ballona Creek, defines a large living area beside the water,bringing new qualities to the residential units. Wetlands (natural park)became an integral part of an urban core,organized as interactive fields or metaballs (attracted surfaces).With this scheme,nature should be both cultivated and "protected ".

23

An international zone starts at the east end of the site,aligned between Jefferson Blvd.and Bluffs and rejuvenated till Lincoln Blvd.and melting together with office,retail,and community service functions.It is a high-tech landscape,akin to an experimental cinema industry,and functions as a double strip 2,5km long,accessible from two linear roads parallel to Jefferson Blvd.A dense rebuilding of the Bluff 's edge blurs and forces equalization at different levels.The strong vectoral orientation of the site runs out at the western part in dispersed low-density recreational facilities and functions.

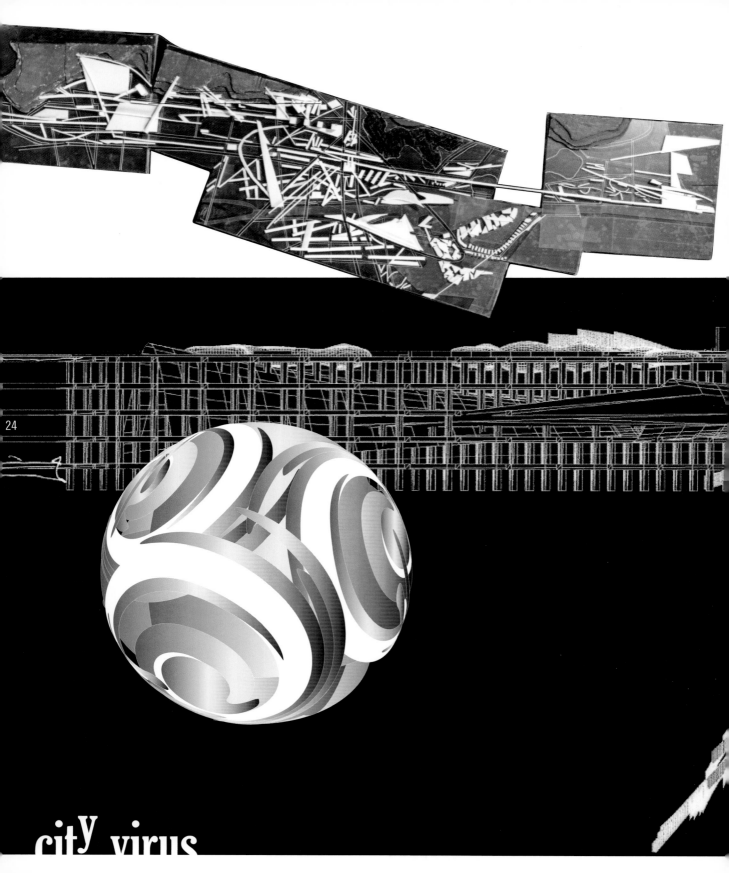

city virus

Finally,a new road network reveals a hierarchical evaluation of built-up territories and voids. This project is both experiment and simulation of possible scenarios for the contemporary city which grows almost simultaneously. The LA-building is a mixture of so many historic styles,from so many influences,that it becomes almost unique."Something completely different " from the elements that have always been there.An image itself, a myth derived from paradoxical ideas.A conglomerate from the schizophrenically more restrictive public space and transparent commercial privateness.Surveillance cameras,private security services —a bunker made of glass.With 5 entrances of which none is the main entrance.With sufficient parking spaces or parking garages,because in Los Angeles buildings are only entered using a car. Los Angeles is the city of the future.The "new city of the twentieth century " has not become a structure of the imagination with gigantic towers,as shown,for example,by Fritz Lang in "Metropolis ".It is the familiar, decentralized world of highways and row houses,shopping centers and office parks which the Americans have created since 1945.

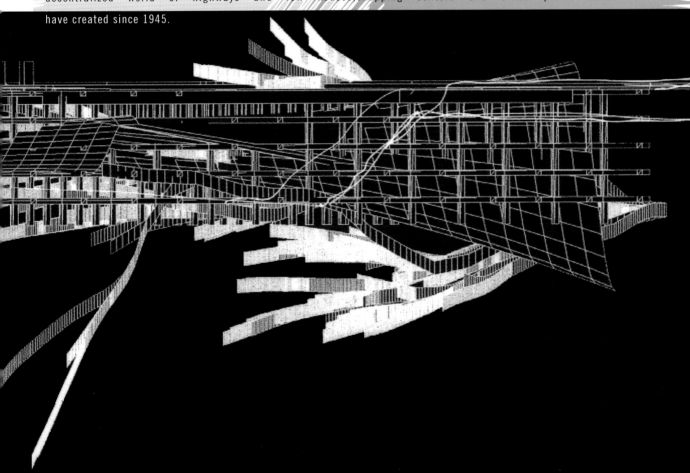

The example of Los Angeles shows clearly that the crucial innovation was the traffic.But streets and cars would not have been able to develop their full revolutionizing effect without the creation of further important new networks of the decentralization:power supply,telecommunication,shopping centers and new methods of business management.The new city is neither urban nor rural nor suburban -it possesses all these elements at the same time. The function of the design is not only to make cities attractive but also to make them more adaptive,more fluid,more capable of accommodating changing demands and unforeseen circumstances. The term landscape invokes the functioning matrix of connective tissue that organizes not only objects and spaces but also the dynamic processes and events that move through them.This is landscape as active surface structuring the conditions for new relationships and interactions among the things its supports.

26

City screenplay

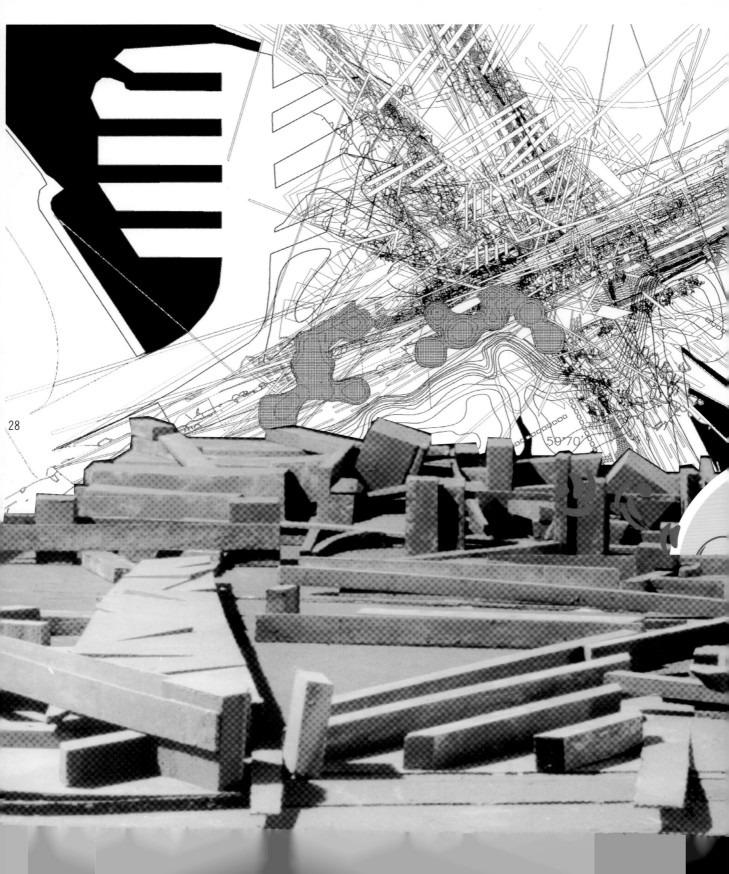

59-70

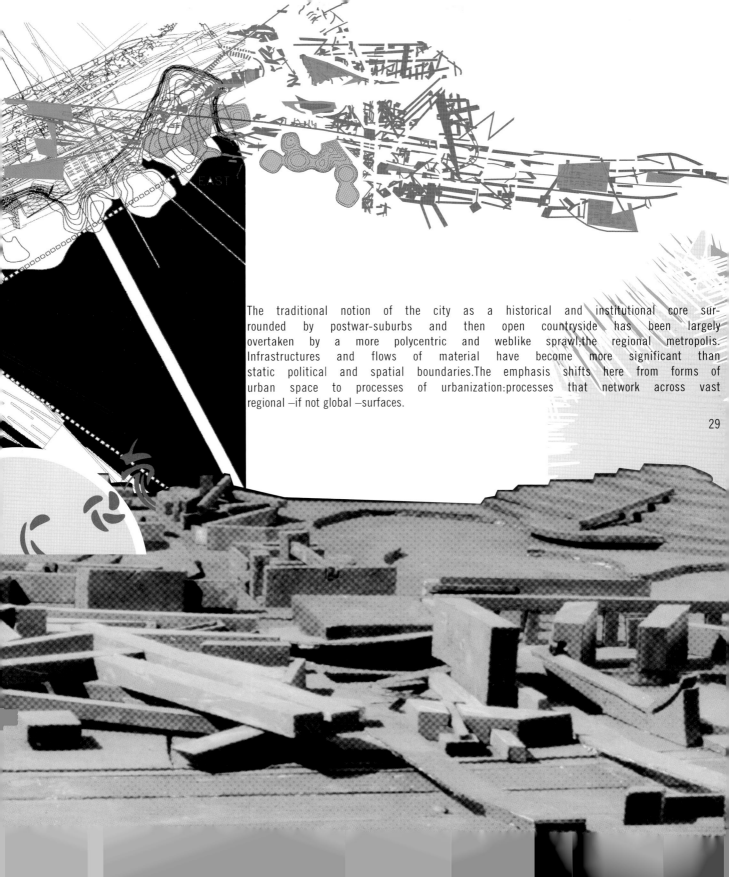

The traditional notion of the city as a historical and institutional core surrounded by postwar-suburbs and then open countryside has been largely overtaken by a more polycentric and weblike sprawl;the regional metropolis. Infrastructures and flows of material have become more significant than static political and spatial boundaries.The emphasis shifts here from forms of urban space to processes of urbanization:processes that network across vast regional —if not global —surfaces.

29

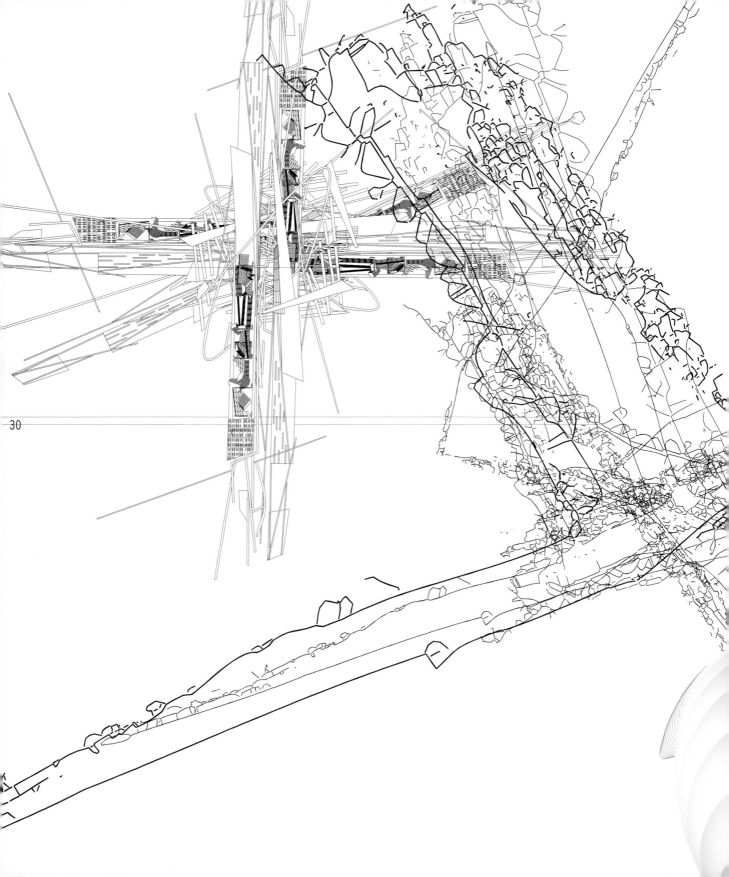

30

A paradigm shift from viewing cities in formal terms to looking at them in dynamic ways.
Hence,familiar urban typologies of square,park,district,and so on are of less use or signifi-
cance than the infrastructures,network flows,ambiguous spaces and other polymorphous
conditions that constitute the contemporary metropolis.
Sociology of the traditional city likes to remind us that social fears are only as a result of
insufficient adaptation to changes.Interesting for us is,however,how the image of Los
Angeles will be treated from a novel about this metropolis to a movie screenplay.

June 16th 2004 was an ordinary day but,neverthe-
less,it has gone down in the history of world archi-
tecture.On this day from eight o 'clock AM until
three

o 'clock in the morning Tula Ferrera experienced the
city of Los Angeles,and the observer got to know
her actions,thoughts and whom she got to meet.
"City at once -Playa Vista ",the city of the century:a
modern adventure without compare.

City at once "Los Angeles " -THE STREET
The language of design,architecture,and urbanism
in Los Angeles is the language of movement.
EXT.DAWN.THE CALIFORNIAN SUN GOES UP.
A long lasting ray hits the camera (flare lens).The
big circle on the horizon moves slowly.It is satu-
rate,

almost artificial,orange light -the city wakes up.
INSERT CARD:"the language of design,architecture,
and urbanism in Los Angeles is the language of
movement.

The typical LA Street.Empty.All the sudden a car
drives by,then an other,and an other,....more and
more,faster and faster.

CUT TO:Traffic jam.Cars all over the place.
Camera flies in between cars.Cars,trucks,pick-ups.
Movement,but slow.

CUT TO:sign on the building.
It says:"Giant city,which has grown almost simultaneously all over,is that all its parts are equal and
equally accessible from all other parts at once ".
The CAMERA starts to move downwards.
As the camera almost reaches the ground the crazy
loop drive begins.Intersected with quick shots of
streets,parking slots,underground parking,parking
structures,and parking big style.Freeway intersec-
tion.The airplane flies over our head.Two cars
crash.

The camera dollies out from the city...we can see a
very big traffic jam,like an endless snake.No people
just cars.

Slow fade out.
CUT TO:Tula Ferrera
The camera on women 's head starts Terry Gilliam 's fly
through and ends up under her ass.
Yes,she is our hero.The adventure starts.It begins and
ends with the street,as all stories in LA.But this is not a
story about the street,it is about the movement.

33

INT.of the car -la skyline:sunset
Palm trees in silhouette against a cherry sky.City lights
twinkle.Los Angeles.A place where anything is pos-
sible.A place where dreams come true.The car slides on
the street.Car turns and enters the helix-parking ramp
and disappears into the building.
INSERT CARD:"Welcome to LA...and have a nice day "
EXT.DUSK
Freeway-scape,drivers ' eye view.
A beautiful golden sun is setting.The sky is on fire.The
CAMERA starts to move downwards.A large neon sign
rises into shot.It rests on top of a sky-scraper and fills the
frame.The building is neither past nor future in design,
but a bit of both.

EXT.HIGH-TECH STRIP
LA –the city of the movies.10 times Blade Runner vision.
Huge theaters floating in the space.A big square,just as
an entrance in total the world of illusions.Gigantic screens
on the buildings make the whole facades dynamic.Drive
of fame.Production and shooting halls.Hardware for
creative production of visions.A little bit too much of
everything.

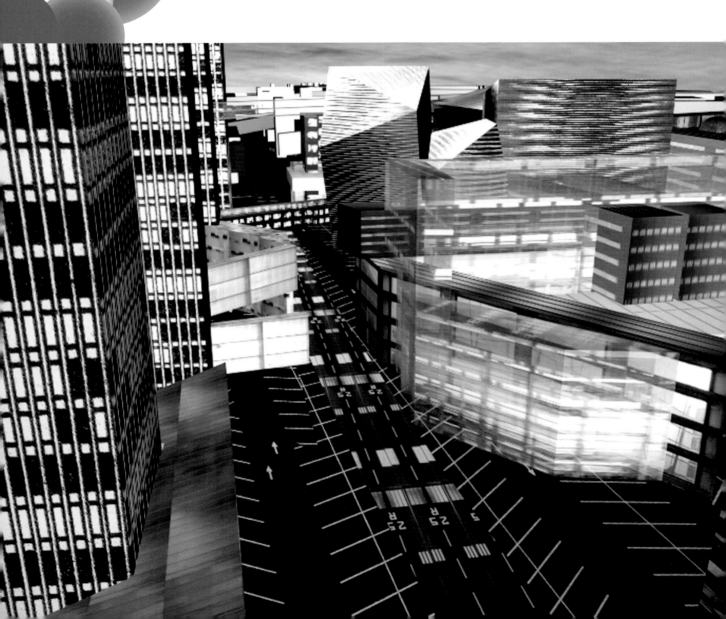

EXT.NIGHT
The city transformed and blurred into sea of lights.
Just lights and neon signs -no buildings any more.
Tula drives toward dark horizon.Slowly we can just
see the reflections of the light in the water.Quick
buzz.The small cabin on the cableway buzzes away
in the lighting speed.
FADE TO BLACK.
City at once "Los Angeles " -THE WAVE
There is a sense in which the beach is the only place
in Los Angeles where all men are equal and on common ground.The culture of the beach is in many
ways a symbolic rejection of the values of the con-
sumer society,a place where a man needs to own
only what he stands up -usually a pair of frayed
shorts and sunglasses.
EXT.DAY -water waves
The nice and smooth Columbian music follows the
waves of the Los Angeles River.The couple of yachts
are moving in groovy rhythm.Camera dolly. Cruising.
CAMERA EXTREME CU:on one burning yacht
The yacht goes in flames.MUSIC CUT:"The roof is on
fire ".
CUT TO:a house with pool A big splash -a la David
Hockney.
CUT TO:Surfboard Fly over with the piece of board in
the corner.WE are fling over the burning yachts,over
the Tula 's head, direct to the beach.Music changes
to "Surfing USA ".

35

the language of design, architecture and urbanism in los angeles is the language of movement

EXT.DAY BEACH

Endless sand shore is full filled with people,take-a-way restaurants.A bunch of artificial islands -a continuous event.A lively and lovely public place.Everybody is happy and dancing.

EXT.SUNSET BEACH

Again one day is over and again the sun goes down.Romantic evening, everything calms down.
FADE TO BLACK.

38

" _At the moment when the digital revolution seems about to melt all that is solid - to eliminate all necessity for concentration and physical embodiment, it seems absurd to imagine the ultimate library, although the future will spell not the end of the book, but the period of new equalities. Revulsion abruptly aborted normal design process and brought us to the idea of rethinking the basic function of library as the storage of hard-copy. Since the invention of writing, libraries were the memory of a culture. But, how to avoid nostalgia for the great central reading room and container of forbidden knowledge?

We developed the notion of reading and walking, or walking and reading, as the conceptual organization of the project. In the theoretically endless space, the program can be extended, programmatic elements (tubes) shifted, and framed again within certain routes. Inspired by literati and the monk's way of reading during medieval times, with the simple thesis that one's concentration and perception is much stronger with movement, the library becomes a very dynamic building. Visitors can receive information or demand video presentations, and walk along reading routes with specific themes.

This project is about a contextless, imaginative and flexible system which describes the narrative space as dualism between the space of reading and the reading of space... the thus occurring cybrid condition does not generate space but a cybrid space can be generated through certain overlaid logics.

Library for the information Age, INTERNET

41_

SPACE

which

are, *for example,* non-hierarchical, nomadic or unstable; dynamic spaces describe juxtapositions of the real and the non real - the notion of displacement. The link between analogue and digital fields concerning the relationship between architecture and virtual media demands new functional and typological concepts:

Our concept of the library revolves around movement - of people, of ideas, of information. Spaces in-between, "media cloths" as projection surfaces for cutting-edge information technology and hardware, defined only by walkways.

This library is not located in a particular place - as an important and positive factor. Its very eccentricity allows it to break away from any static concept. Therefore the concept of the "reading route", in which the endless pursuit of knowledge is supplemented by the pleasure of physical effort.

Four speeds can be achieved in parallel: the speed of one's own body, the mental speed of reading and reflecting on the written information, medial speed for the given environment - automatically adjusted for each user, and an invisible speed of data circulation through digital networks.

The cybrid space can be generated through these overlaid logics. The aim is the de-contextualization and recombination of the media, remediation and new design of knowledge.

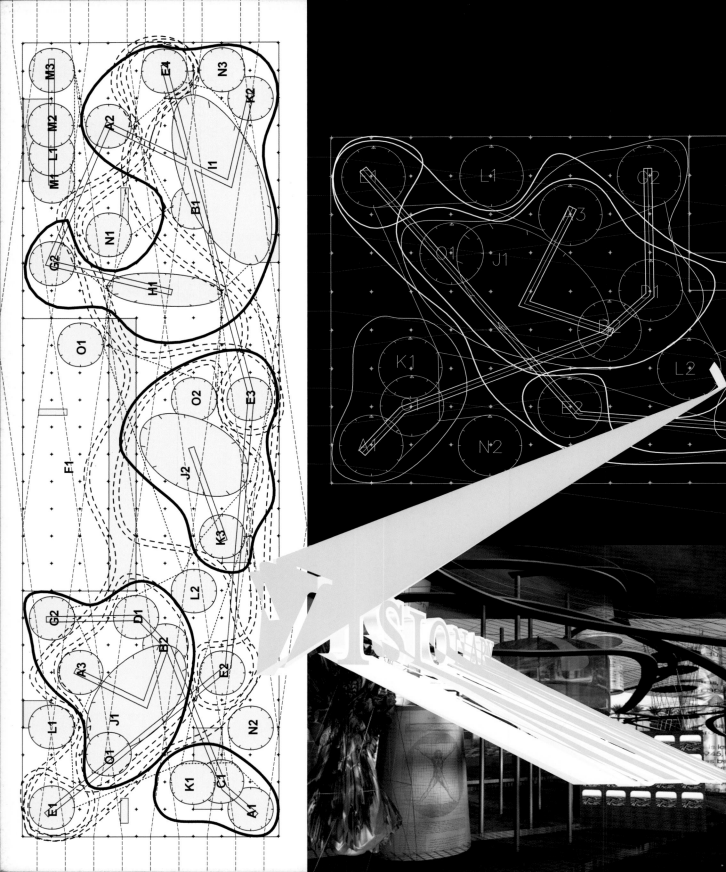

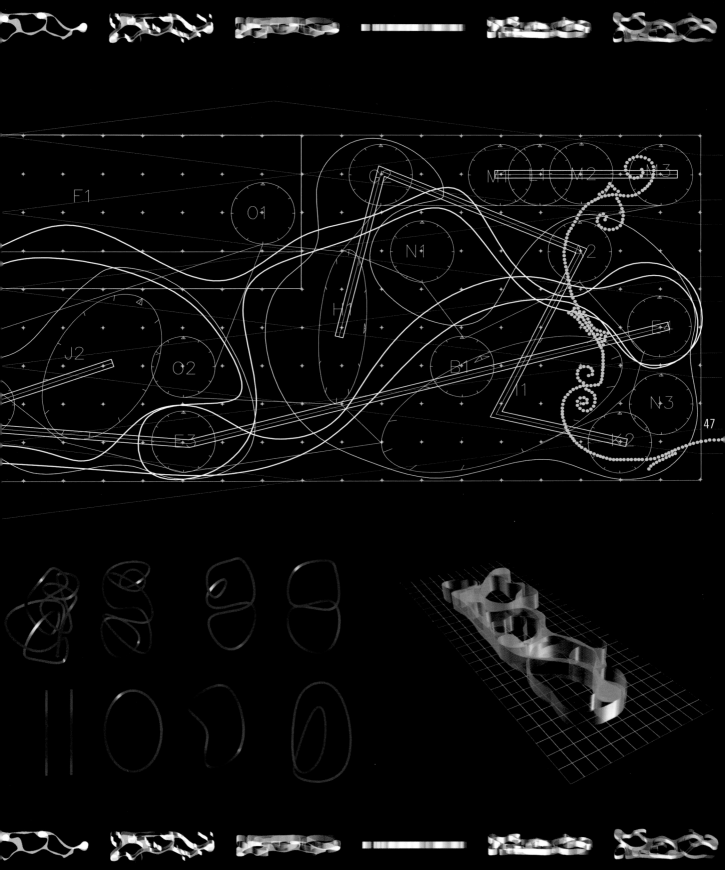

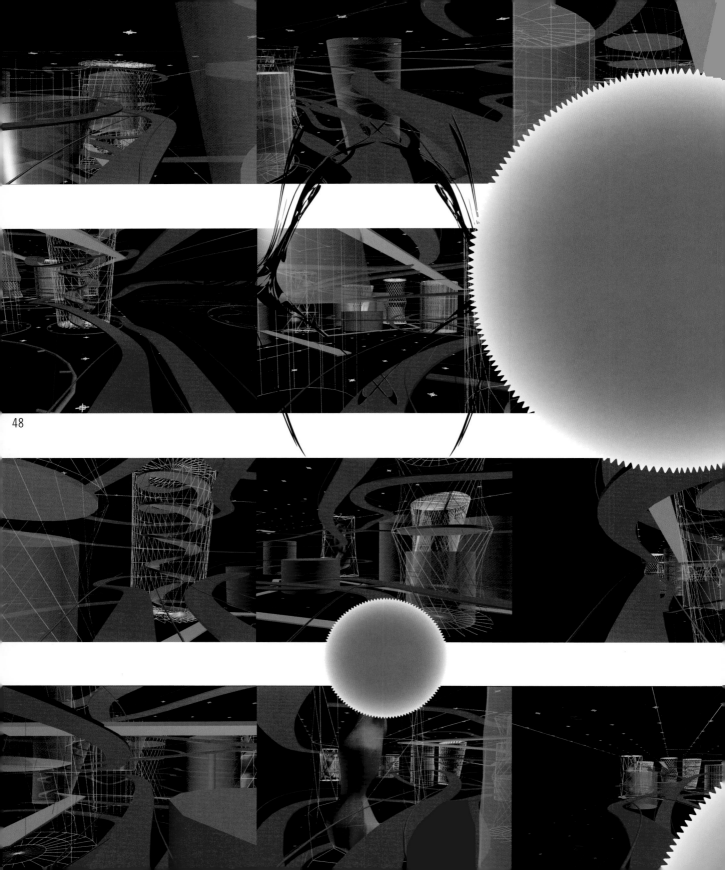

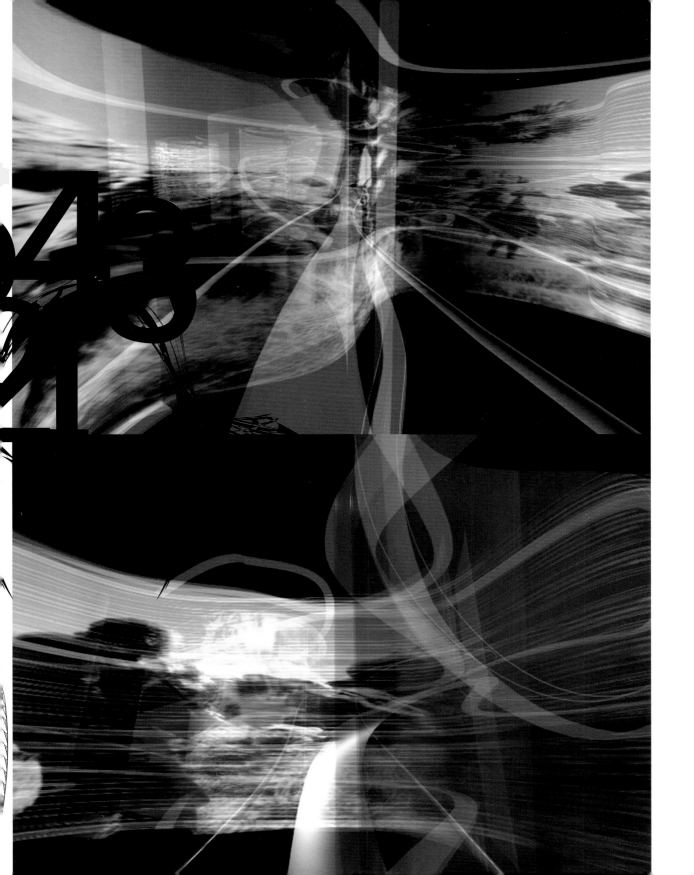

Colas

Ortlos
Venezia, Italy
La Biennale

The conception of our installation

for the exhibition of the 7th International Architecture Exhibition, La Biennale in Venice, with the title of "Less Aesthetics More Ethics", is a symbolic manifesto addressing new methods of operation in architecture. Ortlos translates as 'without space or space off'. It considers work as not dependent on a certain place, but rather in networks, or anywhere where there is connectivity to the web. New working worlds and structures are emerging through this condition. Consequently, the whole process has a strong effect on the actual projects. The object consists of two separate parts, each referring to the 2nd and the 3rd dimension. The projects' boards, representative of classic architectural drawings, are fortified at the side of the lengthwise oriented gangway. The design steps for the respective project are shown. The upper part, a floating, suspended, cloud-like construction consists of 3 video projectors displaying 3d-computer animations - the simulations of the

visions and ideas for an advanced city by the project's "City at Once" and "The library of the information age". It is a form-tube-construction covered with a projection foil which shapes the new frame and defines the space in a space. From the outside the shadows of the viewers and the projections can be seen as a blurry image on the skin. The movement of the visitors through the 'tunnel' is filmed with a video camera and displayed on an external monitor in real time. These images are also broadcast on the Internet. The superimposition of information and movement enables the installation to be experienced in four different ways. The two main topics of ORTLOS are experimental architecture and interface design in urban surroundings. Through the project's "Library for the Information Age", "City at Once", and this installation, we want to raise connections between media-theory and architecture for discussion. This is about the information society in which we live and the virtuality in which we trust, with the aim to simulate and check the real worlds that we are experiencing.

virtual → real

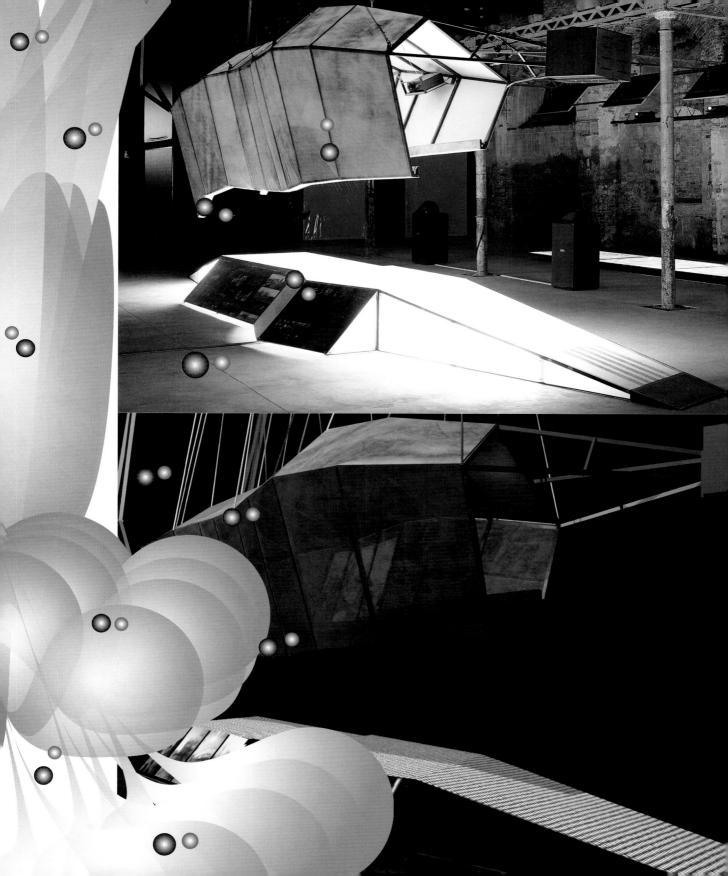

The initial steps in this direction are toward advanced communication and information exchange between users and developers, combined with process-intent generation of complex parametric systems that expand the boundaries of conventional infrastructures. The departure point should be first a simple understanding of the environments that influence our way of life

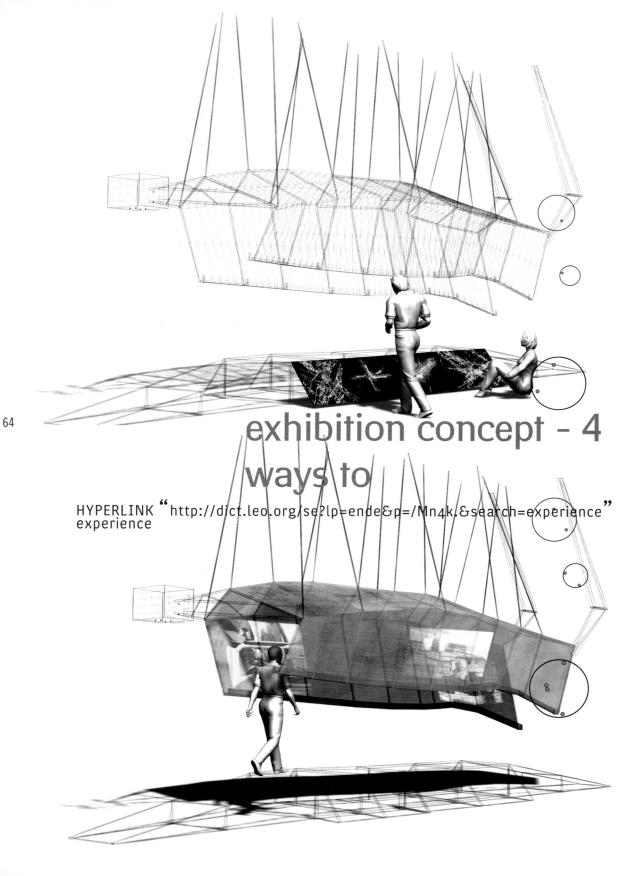

exhibition concept - 4 ways to

HYPERLINK "http://dict.leo.org/se?lp=ende&p=/Mn4k.&search=experience"
experience

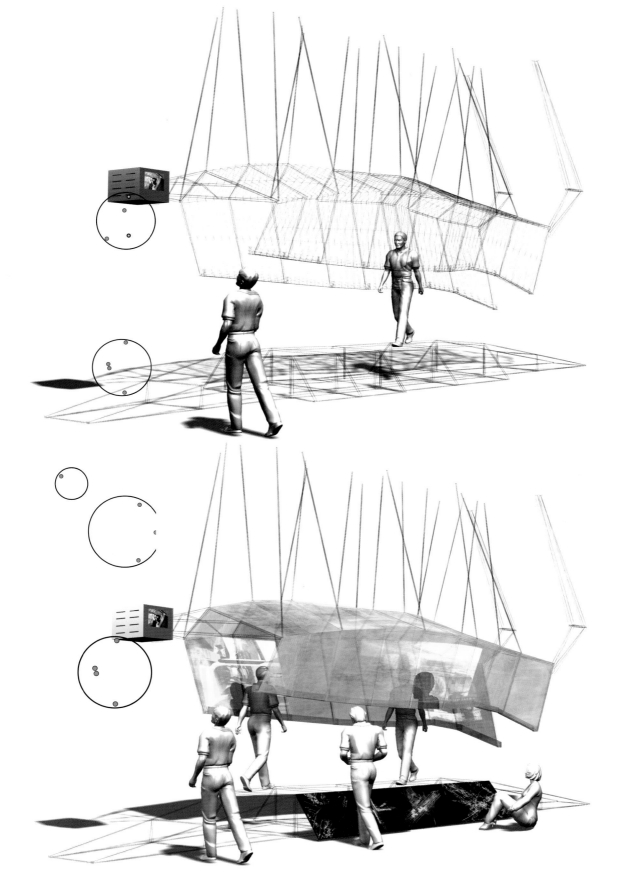

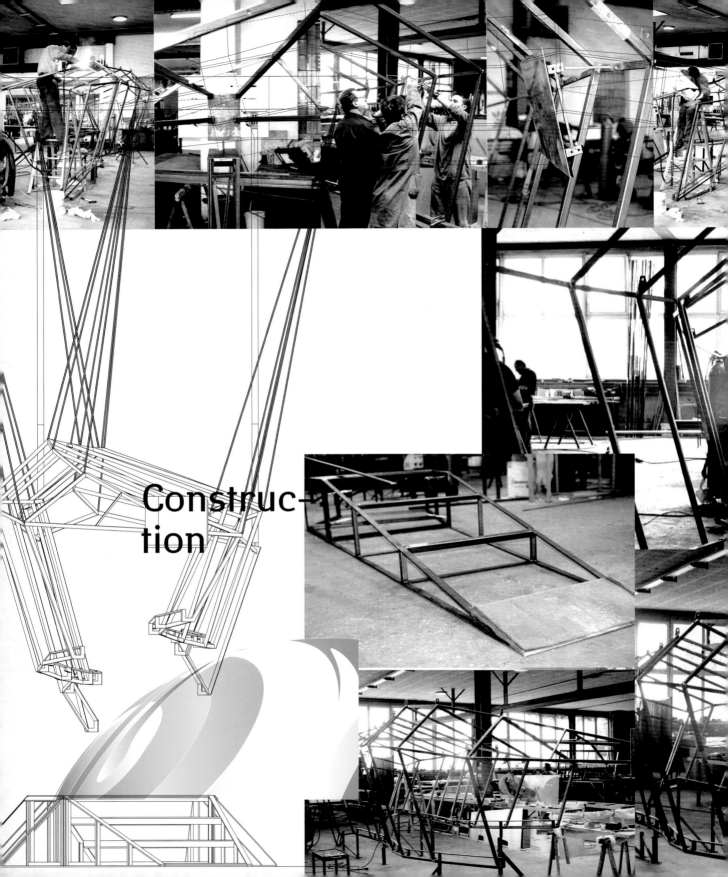

Construc-
tion

67

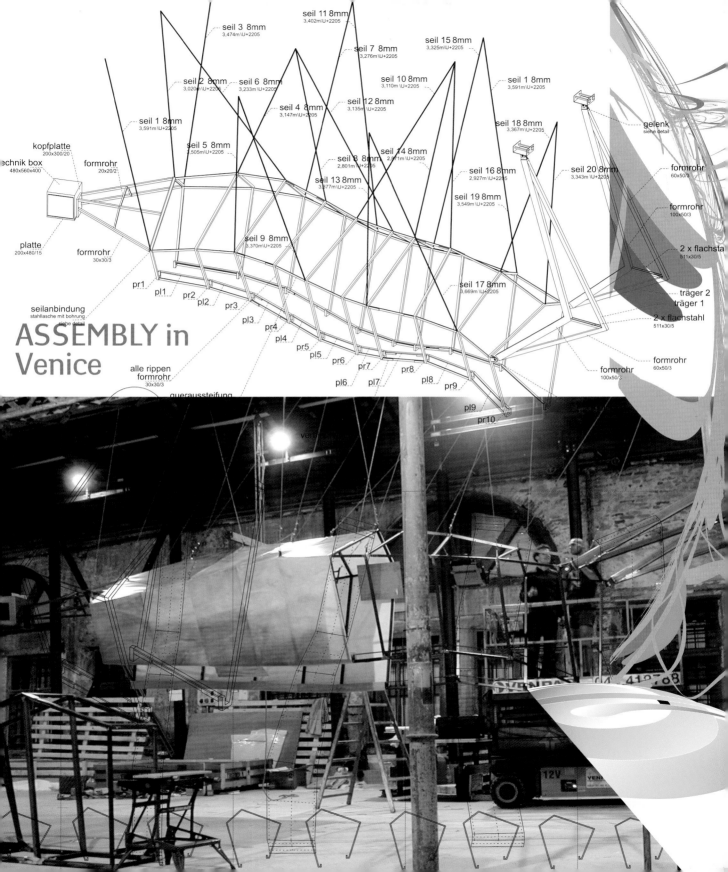

seil 11 8mm
3,402m\U+2205

seil 3 8mm
3,474m\U+2205

seil 7 8mm
3,276m\U+2205

seil 15 8mm
3,325m\U+2205

seil 2 8mm
3,020m\U+2205

seil 6 8mm
3,233m\U+2205

seil 10 8mm
3,110m\U+2205

seil 1 8mm
3,591m\U+2205

seil 4 8mm
3,147m\U+2205

seil 12 8mm
3,135m\U+2205

seil 1 8mm
3,591m\U+2205

seil 5 8mm
3,505m\U+2205

seil 18 8mm
3,367m\U+2205

gelenk
siehe detail

seil 8 8mm
2,801m\U+2205

seil 14 8mm
2,971m\U+2205

seil 16 8mm
2,927m\U+2205

seil 20 8mm
3,343m\U+2205

formrohr
60x50/3

seil 13 8mm
3,877m\U+2205

seil 19 8mm
3,549m\U+2205

formrohr
100x50/3

kopfplatte
200x300/20

technik box
480x560x400

formrohr
20x20/2

2 x flachsta
511x30/5

platte
200x480/15

formrohr
30x30/3

seil 9 8mm
3,370m\U+2205

träger 2
träger 1

2 x flachstahl
511x30/5

seil 17 8mm
3,669m\U+2205

pr1

pl1

pr2

pl2

pr3

formrohr
60x50/3

seilanbindung
stahllasche mit bohrung
siehe detail

pl3

pr4

formrohr
100x50/3

ASSEMBLY in Venice

pl4

pr5

pl5

pr6

pr7

pr8

pr9

alle rippen
formrohr
30x30/3

pl6

pl7

pl8

querausstefung

pl9

pr10

12V

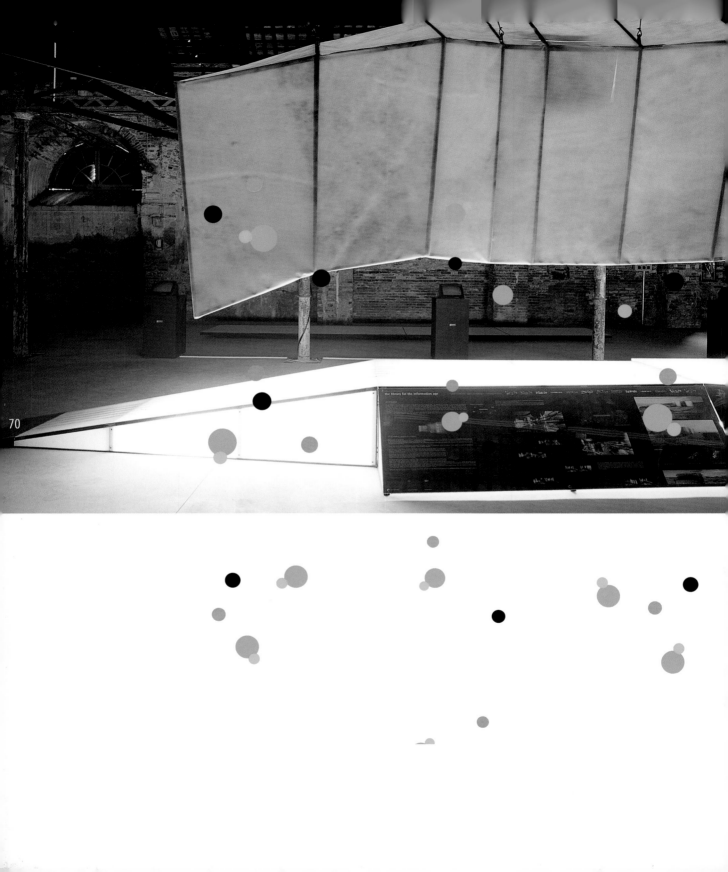

inSPA -
networked space
CEin

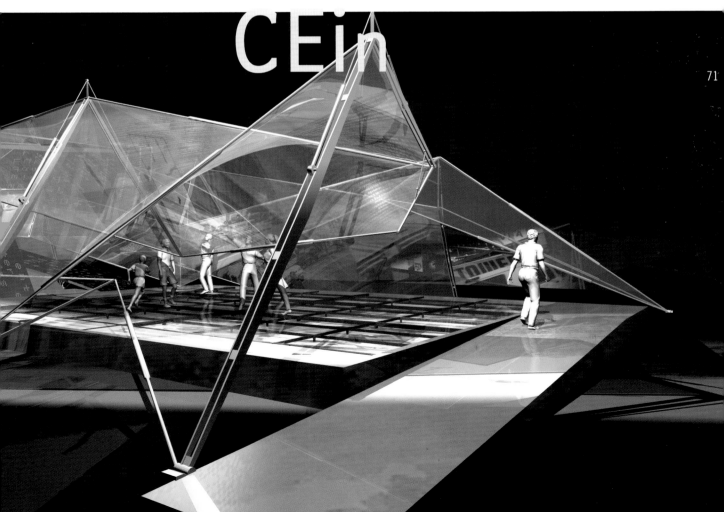

illustration: ai shimizu

vinspace
cell

We want to create an architecturally formulated information-communication environment filled with the cultural content based on
the program for any city. With this installation we are tele-transporting the one urban
atmosphere to the another one.
As a first thought, we define an area in the
area. The superimposition of captured parallel realities and media should occur. "Moving
walls", "Video floor", image projections, "broken information strips" are elements that
should form this area and shape it unpredictably and constantly through change.
So, the space shifts from "moving bodies
through space" into "moving space with bodies". Further on there are space behaviors
and effects which can be activated by sensors
(light, sound, smells, fog, etc). The information that parametrically defines the form
of this area is grasped by telecommunication means, for example – over the Internet
or through input-stations distributed in the
city.

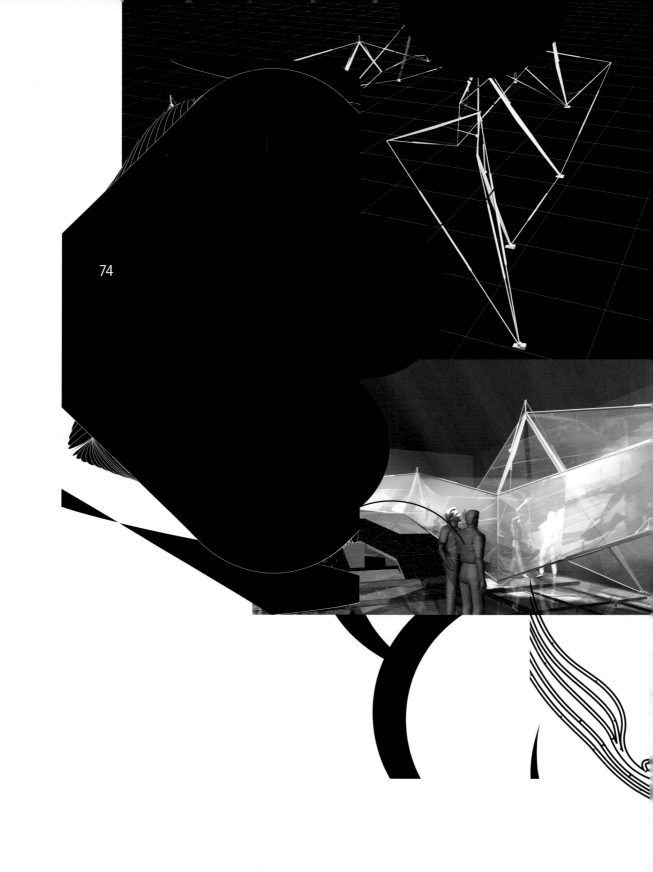

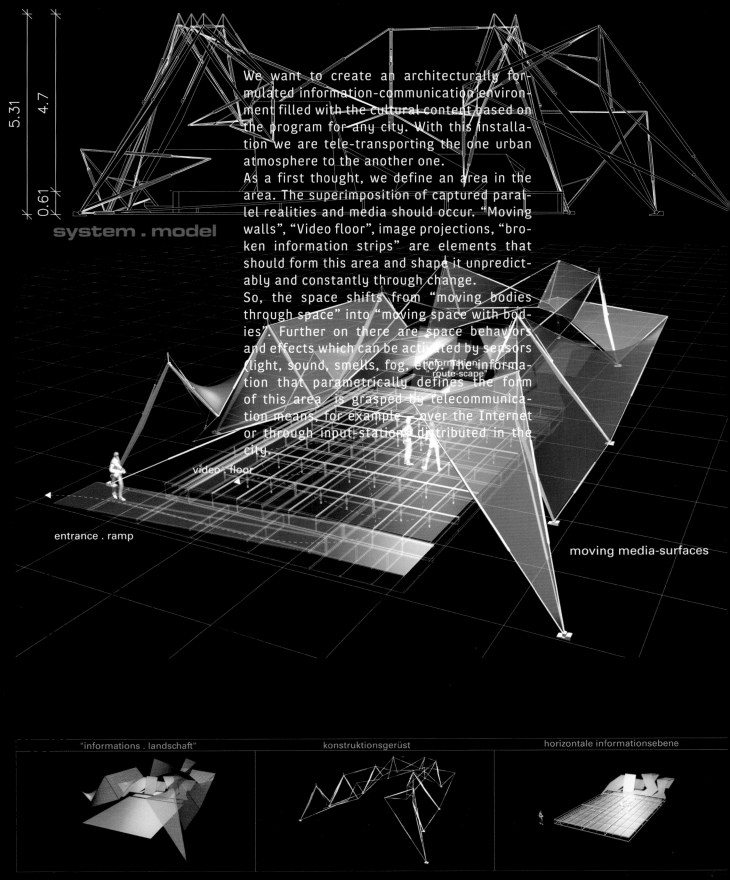

5.31

4.7

0.61

system . model

We want to create an architecturally formulated information-communication environment filled with the cultural content based on the program for any city. With this installation we are tele-transporting the one urban atmosphere to the another one.

As a first thought, we define an area in the area. The superimposition of captured parallel realities and media should occur. "Moving walls", "Video floor", image projections, "broken information strips" are elements that should form this area and shape it unpredictably and constantly through change.

So, the space shifts from "moving bodies through space" into "moving space with bodies". Further on there are space behaviors and effects which can be activated by sensors (light, sound, smells, fog, etc.). The information that parametrically defines the form of this area is grasped by telecommunication means, for example over the Internet or through input-stations distributed in the city.

route-scape

video . floor

entrance . ramp

moving media-surfaces

"informations . landschaft"   konstruktionsgerüst   horizontale informationsebene

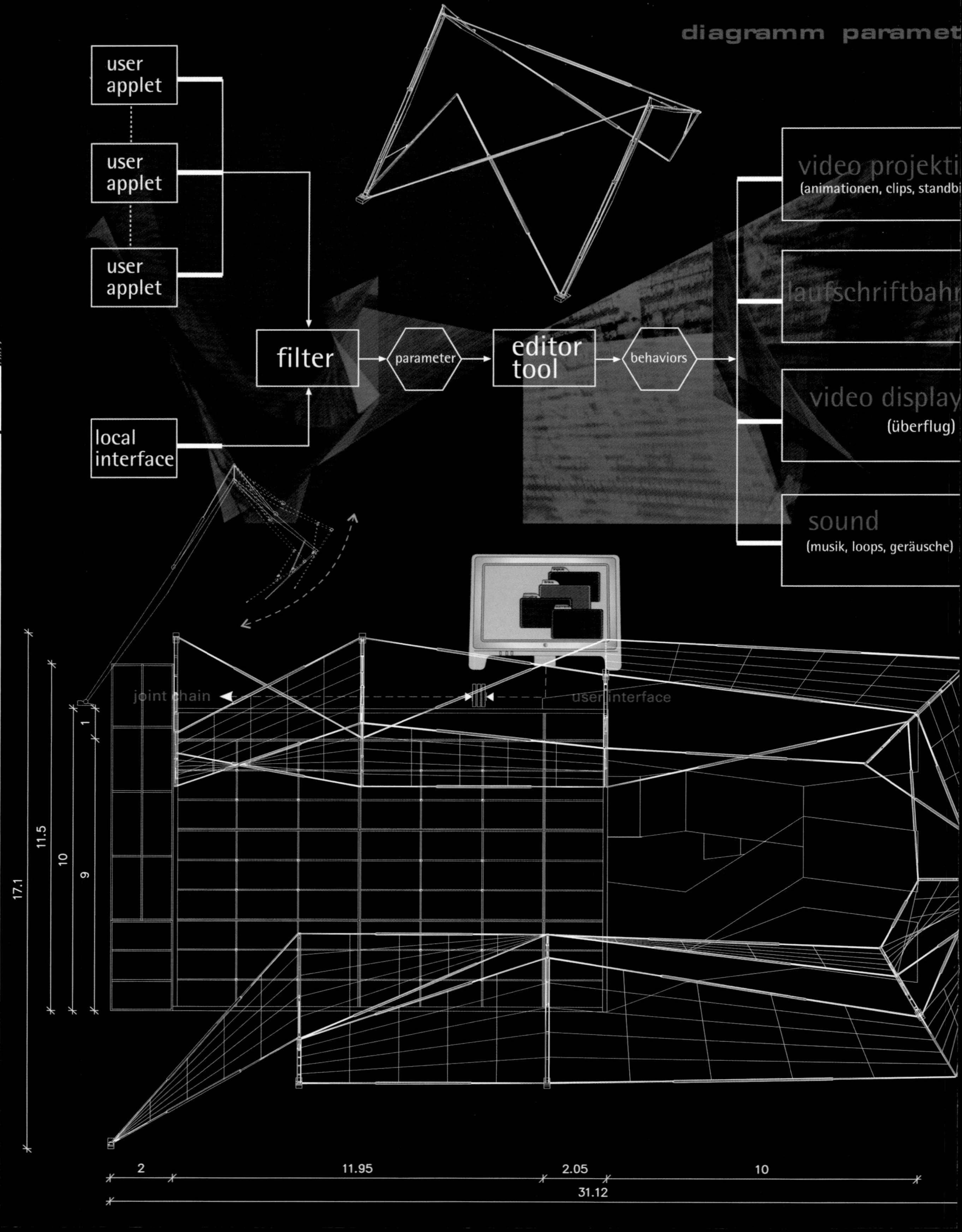

user
applet

user
applet

user
applet

local
interface

filter

parameter

editor
tool

behaviors

video projekti
(animationen, clips, standbi

laufschriftbahr

video display
(überflug)

sound
(musik, loops, geräusche)

joint chain

user interface

76

17.1

11.5

10

9

1

2

11.95

2.05

10

31.12

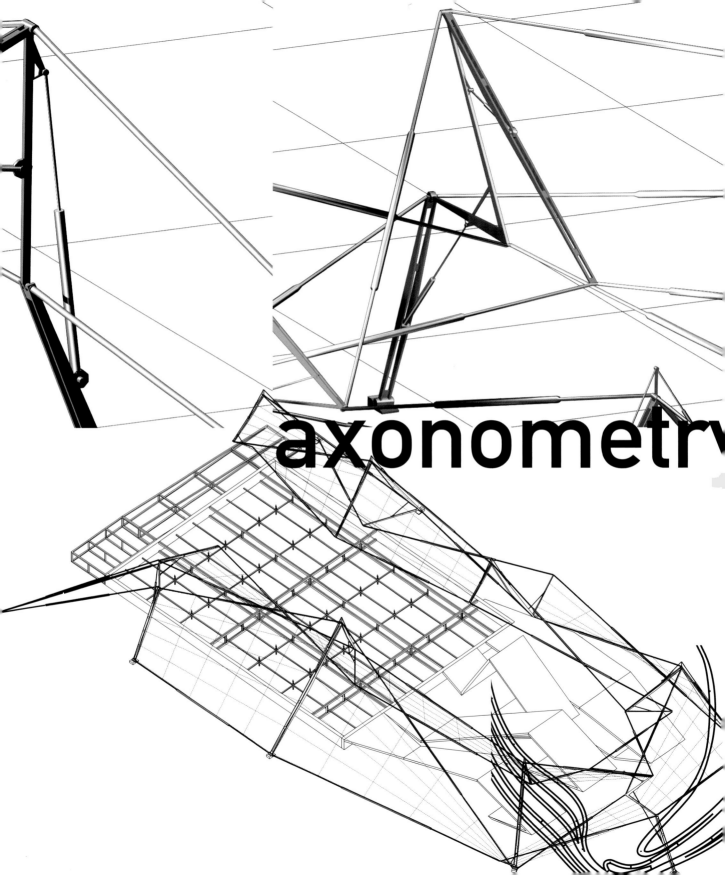

axonometry

profiles

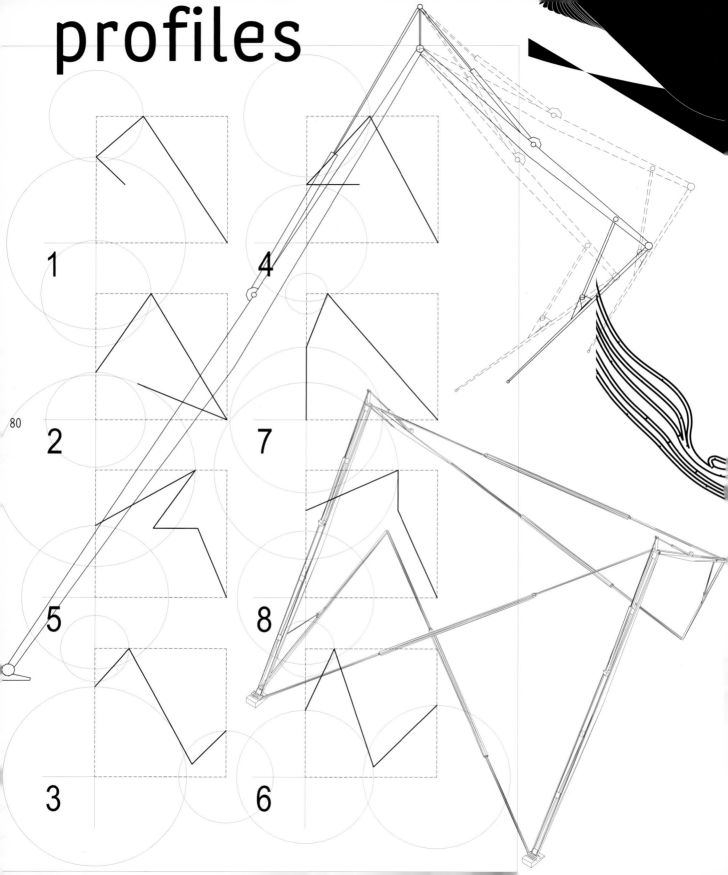

1

4

2

7

5

8

3

6

digital platform A.N.D.I.

transparent   working

process and connections

networked collaboration

a.n.d.i.
a new digital
instrument

Open source architecture, the development and use of A.N.D.I. (A New Digital Instrument for creative networked collaboration) is definitely the most immanent innovative future scenario and will change the situation significantly. This working method will make possible a new generation of projects. It will be an operating system based on the Internet which works interdisciplinarilly and internationally during each architectural or art project to solve complex urban, sociological and architectural problems, to increase the creative dimension of projects, and to improve communication during the process of conception, designing, planning, production and realization of projects.

Main Idea of A.N.D.I.:
A.N.D.I. has two basic features. On the one hand it is a database-driven collaborative environment and on the other hand it will enable the development of future software and tools for networked creative collaboration. This means that A.N.D.I. goes beyond the known B2B concepts, Peer-to-Peer networks or ASP solutions. But the real vision of A.N.D.I. - as an open platform - is only realized if the different tools can be combined together by the users to suit their unique desires and needs. The mission of the A.N.D.I. project is to adapt and evolve the A.N.D.I. platform and associated tools to meet the needs of the tool-building community and its users, so that the vision of A.N.D.I. as an industrial platform can be realized.

A.N.D.I. will develop a virtual office structure in the Internet where its users can work together independent of their location, for the conception, design and production of architectural projects.

It is based on the open source architecture, which means that it is not a final project, but it will also be expanded during the working process to take into consideration experimental architecture, urban planning concepts and interface design.

This digital platform is an operating system, a tool to work at an interdisciplinary and international level during each project but in particular from the very beginning of the design to increase the project's creative dimension.

Additionally, work with this tool will improve communication during the process of designing, planning and realizing architectural projects. This working method

The objective is to develop a run-time environment with the focus on the development of applications for networked international and cross-disciplinary production in the creative sphere of architecture, urban planning and net.art. A.N.D.I. will contribute creative working process by developing an Internet-based operating system, a digital platform for fostering the development of software for interdisciplinary and international collaborations by addressing long term exploratory work. This new working tools will increase the creativity, productivity and competitiveness of the involved actors by drawing upon and developing technologies for virtual, augmented and mixed realities.

82

will enable a new generation of architectural and art projects concerning authorship, creative input (to use the computer not just for representation but as a design tool), and non-expected output. The project is not developed by individuals but in collaboration with an interdisciplinary and international team of experts from different areas.

The platform *A.N.D.I.* is a digital working instrument. It's a ready-made constantly-changing infrastructure that can be shared by project partners. The main user interface will *have 4 main modules:*

1. INFOSPACE: this is the actual input of unfiltered information from interdisciplinary users. Cognitive map knowledge consists of information concerning spatial relations and data on environmental characteristics, and allows people to successfully operate within this virtual environment and process data.

2. Communication and content management: information flow and start of interaction between the project partners.

3. AWSP – active work server **pages**: A.N.D.I. engine, working place, always changing and growing dependent on the working progress, internal visualization of the collaborative work, design visualization tools, presentation utilities for the virtual meeting, ideas generator .

4. Database: all modules are connected to the databases which can be queried from every stage of the design process. Documentation of processes, and presentation of projects.

start user interfaces of Active Work Server Pages (AWSP)← ←

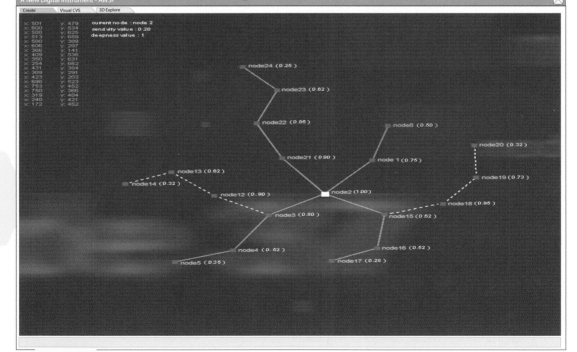

Initially, "a.n.d.i"

will address a group of people and partners who are highly motivated and looking for individual ways of participating and intervening in their local and global urban situations. Main actors will be architects, urban planners, net artists, sociologists, media theorists, technology partners and developers, economy experts, production firms, service companies, and last but not least – clients. The ultimate objective and our vision will be to bring all those users together and create the virtual working space for the projects in their first creative conceptual phase.

input
of the
build.
ers

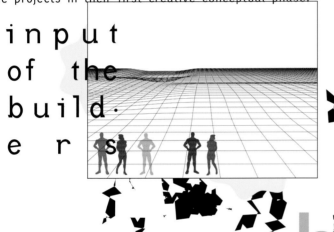

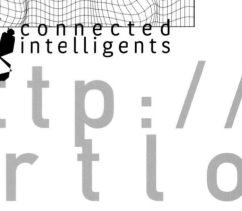

connected
intelligents

84

http://
ortlo

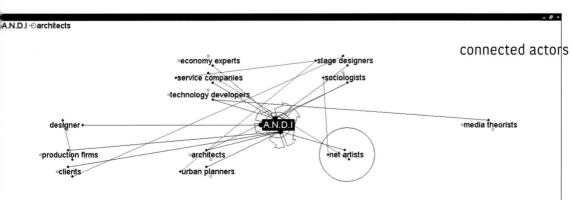

A.N.D.I -⊖architects

connected actors

°economy experts   •stage designers

•service companies   •sociologists

◦technology developers

designer•   A.N.D.I   ◦media theorists

◦production firms   •architects   •net artists

◦clients   •urban planners

◦logy developers ▢ economy experts ▢ production firms ▢ designer ▢ service companies ▢ clients ▢ stage designers ▢ sociologists ▢ architects ▢ A.N.D.I ✕

flow of the information

Task statement

Nowadays, traditional architecture is less and less capable of giving competent answers to many complex questions. Current architectural discourse declares architecture as dead, which gives a great opportunity to declare a new beginning. Actually, "the innovation" in the new architecture is a paradigm switch in the domain of working methods. Trans-local and network-oriented environment force you to think and work in a different way, and new results will be produced.

The first steps in this direction are as follows: improved communication between the user and the developer, as well as the generation of complex systems of parametrical procedural decisions.

The changes of architectural production are linked to changes in thinking about architecture and architectural practice. A work will no longer be an expression of a single individual; it is an expression of the collective. More – it is an expression of a platform – one of a network of influences which are continuously being reorganized by all the participants involved.

According to the present market situation, big companies acquire huge projects because of their size and power. They are at the same time very slow and inflexible, with high costs invested in the infrastructure. Small firms (one-man businesses and small offices) are flexible but they don't have enough resources and sufficient infrastructure for bigger projects. Medium-sized firms are flexible but not big enough to be serious competition in the long term. Pre-investment is also connected to high risks.

One of the most frequent problems of architecture production is the loss of information between planner and producer and the final process of building. It is necessary to make the design process transparent and immediate for all involved project partners (designer, producer, developer and clients).

Apart from the reduction of the project costs through shared and already developed infrastructure and mobility of the working place the planning process becomes more transparent and understandable for the clients due to the permanent up-to-date simulation and 3d-visualisation of every stage of the design progress.

This platform should give the designers and all team members a new tool – not only for use with new working methods, but also to make possible unforeseen results and bring about new qualities in the field of architectural design and urban planning as one of the most important preconditions for creating our future physical (real) and (influence)

www.
s.at

The project aim is to cross over the existing borders in collaborative environments where ideas and intensive creative work done by artists and architects encounters state-of-the-art information and communication technologies (ICT). In such a setting, ICT is used beyond mere data and information processing to enable idea sharing, creativity and interaction. The process is very complex in a sense that integrates multiple aspects of the problem, including heterogeneous data formats, idea representation and communication, creative design process support, interaction and collaboration support, automatic mapping of the problem aspects onto software architecture, identification of value-creation nets within the process, and business models and mechanisms for successful dissemination on the global market. Hence, conceptual design and development of such a platform require a unique combination of specific knowledge and experience to successfully conduct integral research and development in the fields of software architecture, communication middleware, web programming, OO design, formal models, knowledge representation and engineering, meta programming, software tools development, ontologies, process models, and formal business modeling.

Technical elements:

The central technical element consists of a system development approach. It includes both the operating system itself and the user interface. The general features are fixed first in a conceptual phase, and then more and more details are added. The system architecture to be defined in the system-modeling phase is open, and a modular concept is chosen from the beginning, with clear and well-defined interfaces between the modules. This method makes it possible to add and/or configure system modules to the system in an easy, fast and cheap way, thus providing attractive solutions for applications which represent an alternative to the standard approach. The application development will be executed with state-of-the-art tools.

The technology used beyond the user interface is based on up-to-date web-oriented applications. This aspect has its main advantage in working on platform-independent environments. This means that users will be able to make inputs, to share and to process data through commonly used internet browser software extended with freeware or low-cost shareware available plug-ins. Since the operating system, the database, the scripts and every step of the design development are server-side included, the user can log in and use his workstation connected to the Internet more or less as a terminal with a default configuration. This saves user's money and time for software installation, technical support and expensive hardware. The local interface should be adaptable to the user's own preferences, irrespective of place or time of login, and thus confer more flexibility concerning work practice, allowing them to concentrate on the actual work.

```
package org.apache.jsp;

import javax.servlet.*;
import javax.servlet.http.*;
import javax.servlet.jsp.*;
import org.apache.jasper.runtime.*;

public class RepositoryAdminView$jsp extends HttpJspBase {

    // begin [file="/RepositoryAdminView.jsp";from=(5,0);to=(5,76)]
    // end

    static {
    }
    public RepositoryAdminView$jsp( ) {
    }

    private static boolean _jspx_inited = false;

    public final void _jspx_init() throws org.apache.jasper.runtime.JspException {
    }

    public void _jspService(HttpServletRequest request, HttpServletResponse response)
        throws java.io.IOException, ServletException {

        JspFactory _jspxFactory = null;
        PageContext pageContext = null;
        HttpSession session = null;
        ServletContext application = null;
        ServletConfig config = null;
        JspWriter out = null;
        Object page = this;
        String __value = null;
        try {

            if (_jspx_inited == false) {
                synchronized (this) {
                    if (_jspx_inited == false) {
                        _jspx_init();
                        _jspx_inited = true;
                    }
                }
            }
            _jspxFactory = JspFactory.getDefaultFactory();
            response.setContentType("text/html;charset=ISO-8859-1");
            pageContext = _jspxFactory.getPageContext(this, request, response,
                                        "", true, 8192, true);

            application = pageContext.getServletContext();
            config = pageContext.getServletConfig();
            session = pageContext.getSession();
            out = pageContext.getOut();

            // HTML // begin [file="/RepositoryAdminView.jsp";from=(0,0);to=(5,0)]
            out.write("<!DOCTYPE HTML PUBLIC \"-//W3C//DTD HTML 4.0 Transitional//EN\">\r\n<html
equiv=expires content=\"\">\r\n");

            // end
            // begin [file="/RepositoryAdminView.jsp";from=(5,0);to=(5,76)]
            controlcenter.DataBean dataBean = null;
            boolean _jspx_specialdataBean = false;
            synchronized (session) {
                dataBean= (controlcenter.DataBean)
                pageContext.getAttribute("dataBean",PageContext.SESSION_SCOPE);
                if ( dataBean == null ) {
                    _jspx_specialdataBean = true;
                    try {
                        dataBean = (controlcenter.DataBean) java.beans.Beans.instantiate(this.getClass().ge
                    } catch (ClassNotFoundException exc) {
                        throw new InstantiationException(exc.getMessage());
                    } catch (Exception exc) {
                        throw new ServletException (" Cannot create bean of class "+"controlcenter.DataBe
                    }
                    pageContext.setAttribute("dataBean", dataBean, PageContext.SESSION_SCOPE);
                }
            }
            if(_jspx_specialdataBean == true) {
            // end
            // begin [file="/RepositoryAdminView.jsp";from=(5,0);to=(5,76)]
            }
            // end
            // HTML // begin [file="/RepositoryAdminView.jsp";from=(5,76);to=(21,0)]
            out.write("\r\n<script language=\"javascript\" src=\"/script/ua.js\"></script>\r\n<script L
xbStyle.js\"></script>\r\n<script LANGUAGE=\"JavaScript\" SRC=\"/script/xbCollapsibleLists.js\"></s
22;\r\nvar bgColor =\"#CCCCCC\";\r\nvar font1h =\"<FONT FACE='Arial,Helvetica' SIZE=-1'><B>\";\
\"</FONT>\";\r\n");

            // end
            // begin [file="/RepositoryAdminView.jsp";from=(21,3);to=(21,30)]
            out.print(dataBean.getSingleData()[2]);
            // end
            // HTML // begin [file="/RepositoryAdminView.jsp";from=(21,32);to=(36,36)]
            out.write("\r\nbl.build(10, 10);\r\n}\r\nfunction redo(){document.location.reload();}\r\n// --><
css\">\r\n</head>\r\n<BODY text=#000000 bgColor=#B9D6DA onload=init() class=\"main_text\">\r
width=\"233\" height=\"43\">    <span class=\"head1\">Repository</span> \r\n

            // end
            // begin [file="/RepositoryAdminView.jsp";from=(36,39);to=(36,66)]
            out.print(dataBean.getSingleData()[0]);
            // end
            // HTML // begin [file="/RepositoryAdminView.jsp";from=(36,68);to=(53,10)]
            out.write("</span> \r\n       <HR size=\"1\" noshade>\r\n      <span class=\"m
<TABLE>\r\n      <TBODY> \r\n      <TR> \r\n      <TH></TH>\r\n
table\">Description  </TH>\r\n       <TH align=\"left\" nowrap class=\"head-table\">
TH>\r\n       <TH align=\"left\" nowrap class=\"head-table\">Owner  </TH>\r\n

            // end
            // begin [file="/RepositoryAdminView.jsp";from=(53,12);to=(53,64)]
            for (int i=0; i<dataBean.getRowData().size(); i++){
            // end
            // HTML // begin [file="/RepositoryAdminView.jsp";from=(53,66);to=(56,52)]
            out.write("\r\n      <tr> \r\n       <td> \r\n       <input type=
```

It is in the nature of the project to use technologies which are platform independent (like Java2, CVS Java servlets & JSP Engine for example), and to use already-gained knowledge of existing open source projects (like for example Jakarta project with its sub-projects: the goal of the Jakarta Project is to provide commercial-quality server solutions based on the Java Platform that are developed in an open and cooperative fashion.).

Technology Concept Definition - Database/Code model concept

Data organization is divided among several modules

- system
- information
- information management
- communication
- project management

Each module has its business level and end-user level implementation using following technologies:

- Java Beans
- JSP/Servlet
- Java Applets

The system module implements required data for managing users, security topics, serialization options and repository administration. The information module covers work-data storage (database/file-system) and external data in use (distributed network data). The information management module represents advanced mathematical functions for intuitive info-relation modification and usage. The concept is based on the technologies of fuzzy logic and neural networks which implement heuristic methods of conclusion. The communication module stores data needed for collaborative work and synchronization among participants. The project management module is conceptually based on the information module and covers the step of implementation and development (time sheets, financial topics, workflow organization).

Innovation-related activities

The system,

communication, information and project management modules are the shell (operating system) tools. Those are the bases for modules that represent technological advance.

The main research is in the fields of information management and active interfaces. Both are self-developing structures and require modular implementation adequate for modifications during both test phase and exploitation phase.

Making conclusions or getting the unexpected output is the problem that involves complex heuristic calculations. Technologies required for solving them are based on mathematical logic (fuzzy logic), neural networking and numeric mathematical calculations. 99 percent of output generation tasks are without enough input data, or with data that may or may not be relevant for the problem the end-user has. Impact of the data itself is gained from all work interfaces. Methods regarding this data management have common interfaces used by these work interfaces.

The research in this area is based on developing input/output methods for active and visual representation for dynamic manipulated data.

A New Digital Instrument - AWSP

Create   Visual CVS   3D Explore

3D Navigation - Java + OpenGL

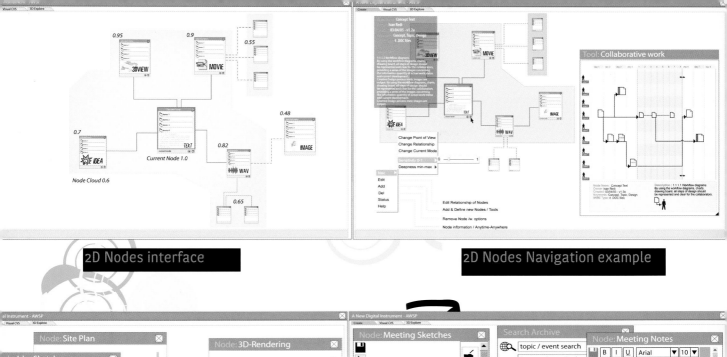

2D Nodes interface

2D Nodes Navigation example

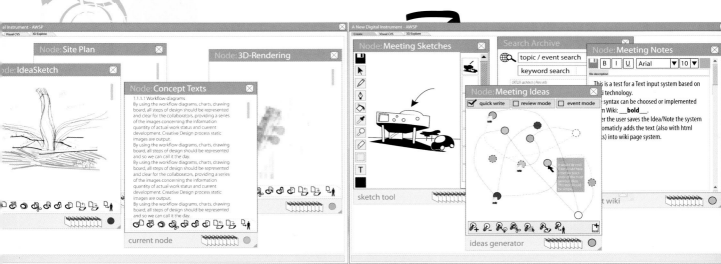

Zoom-In nodes

Tools

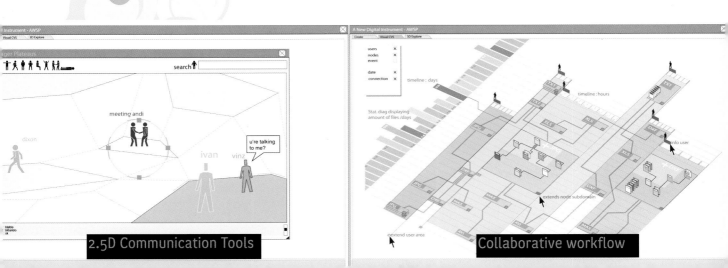

2.5D Communication Tools

Collaborative workflow

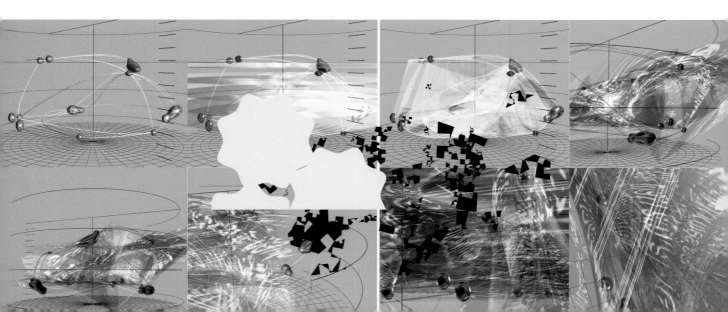

THE GRAND EGYPTIAN MUSEUM

giza, egypt

The crucial and central question is how to build a museum which is strong enough to bear comparison with the pyramids. **A superb task.**

Our project for the Grand Egyptian Museum attempts to present and visualize the country's great history rather than to show the exhibits only. The objects become more understandable when they can be viewed in the context of the everyday life of ancient civilizations (the highest level of education back then, was received in the so-called "houses of life"). The image of our project is based on the tension between fluidity vs. materiality, dynamic vs. static, open vs. closed.

There is no up or down. The building - like a city - completely surrounds us: the virtual structures of the museum are connected with each other at every conceivable angle; there is no horizon either; the mesh of building-like shapes stretches in all directions. Unlike the commercial spaces of the net, which had carefully enforced certain real-world rules such as horizon and perspective, the museum seems to have turned its back on petty Newtonian conventions.

daylight radiosity

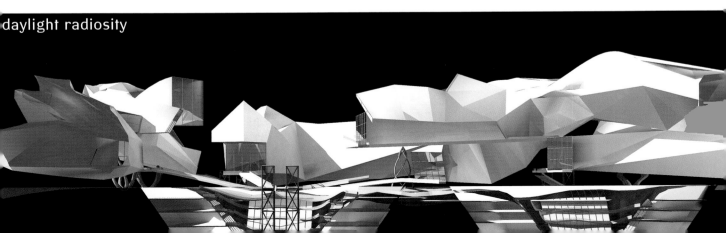

urban situation

The museum is situated on the highest point of the site and is perceptible from all approaching directions. The decision to concentrate the museum complex on the quadratic area eastwards and not to occupy the whole site provides unique possibilities: the site can be organized in a logical, clear manner and allow further extensions even with the structures not directly connected to the proposed buildings supporting the idea of modularity - all this in an urban concept. The museum "searches" for the urbanity on the west side and provides a grand view from the northeast side. Additionally it opens itself southwards towards pyramids.

The zoning of the site takes three main functions into consideration:
1)   Arrival to the site by any means of transportation from the east side (private cars, buses, and public transportation) and parking;
2)   Approaching the museum, from the parking lots, either by foot or by internal transportation system (ideally small buses powered by solar energy) through the first theme park - dunal park;
3)   And the museum complex itself.

The employees and the deliverers access the complex from the service street on the west side. The zoning regulation is based on organizational lines and axes applied to the displaced surface which is a main carrier for the distribution of the program, under the consideration of the existing terrain. In addition the public spaces, circulation network, open-air exhibitions and theme parks support the idea of openness of the concept.

design development

The investigation of the site brought us to the conclusion that we need a main organizational landscape (what we call a displaced surface - geometric deformation based on the density of the program-information particles), which defines the reference datum for the vertical shift of the program: under the surface, the surface itself and above the surface.

The actual museum building mass restricts itself to the area 300m by 300m, which is approximately the base area of the great pyramid. This quadrate is rotated by 45degrees with respect to the pyramids' orientation.

The main program exhibition topics are connected to the so-called bone system, which allows every shift and movement of one program element to influence the whole system (inverse kinematics). This makes it possible to solve complex organizational systems. The ends of these bone elements are brought to 5 neural points and represent later connections to the infrastructural network.

The flow simulation of the program and visitors also give us some new information about possible unforeseen connections between the spaces and users.

Finally, the spaces (exterior and interior) are functionally and organizationally designed to yield the most quality for the further uses.

splaced surface / shape of a pyramid & the new program / the bones system / the real flow simulation / the flow mesh / optimized form & begin of the final design

URBAN VIEW - LOOKING TOWARD PYRAMIDS

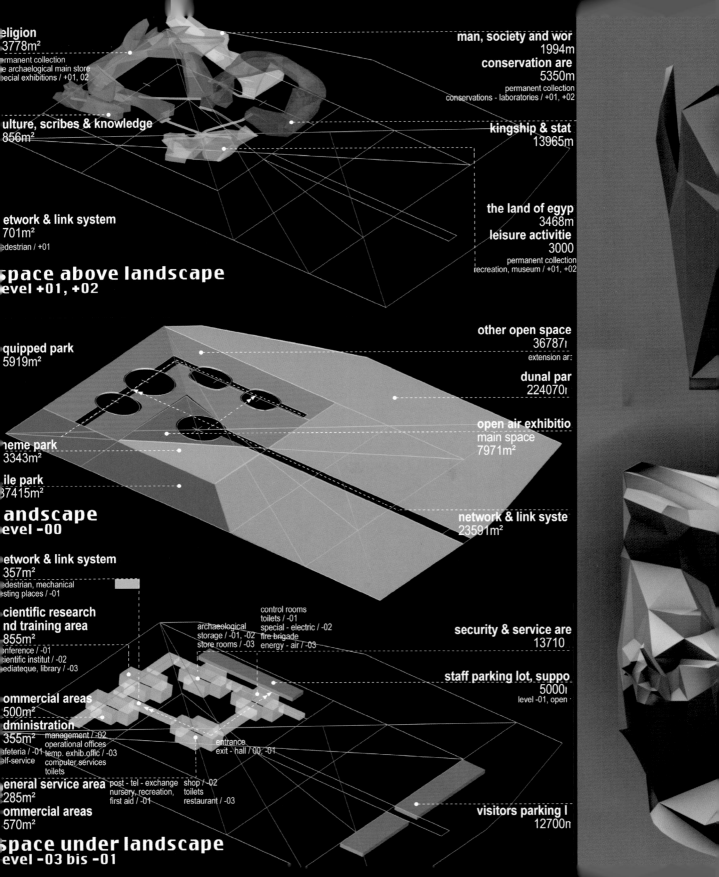

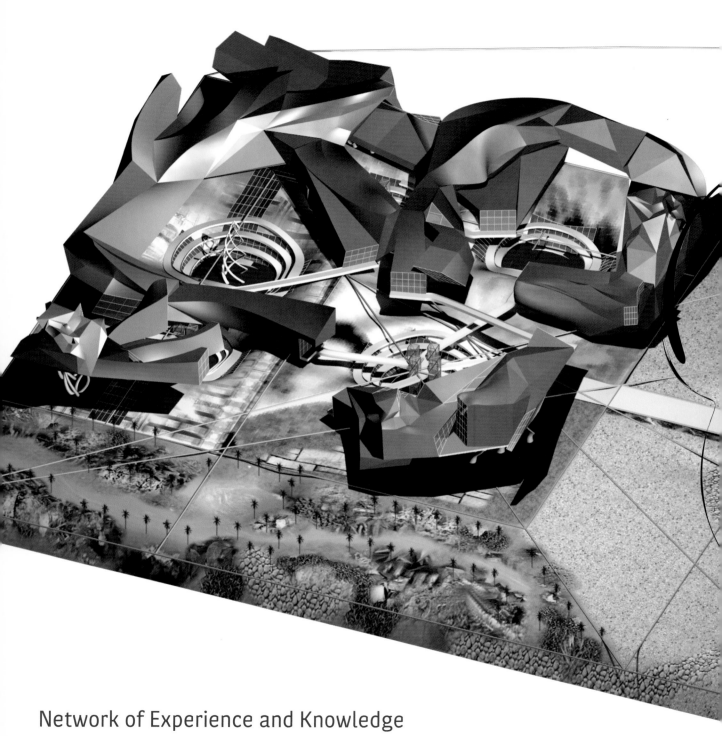

Network of Experience and Knowledge

Building and Landscape $\rightarrow\rightarrow$ Information surface = Knowledge Landscape

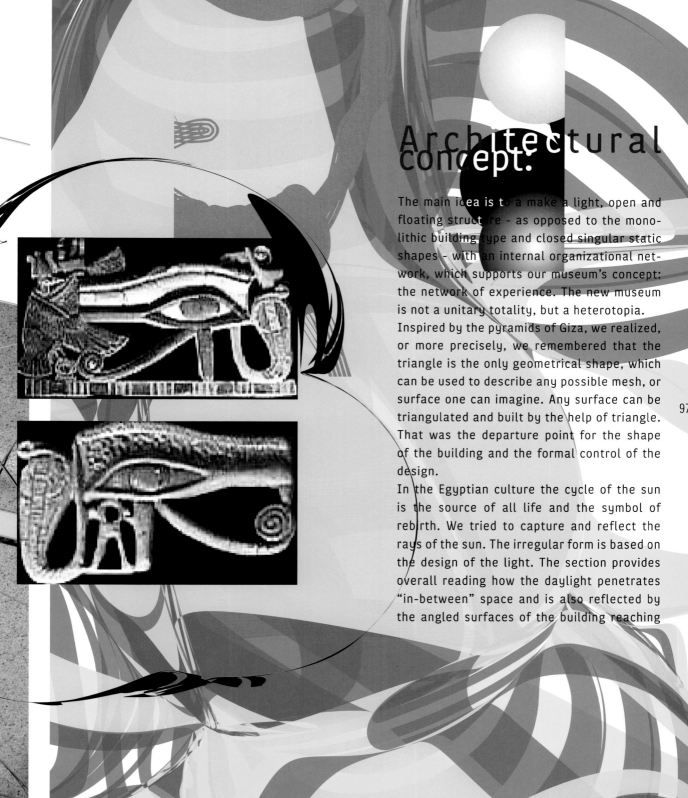

Architectural concept:

The main idea is to a make a light, open and floating structure - as opposed to the monolithic building type and closed singular static shapes - with an internal organizational network, which supports our museum's concept: the network of experience. The new museum is not a unitary totality, but a heterotopia.

Inspired by the pyramids of Giza, we realized, or more precisely, we remembered that the triangle is the only geometrical shape, which can be used to describe any possible mesh, or surface one can imagine. Any surface can be triangulated and built by the help of triangle. That was the departure point for the shape of the building and the formal control of the design.

In the Egyptian culture the cycle of the sun is the source of all life and the symbol of rebirth. We tried to capture and reflect the rays of the sun. The irregular form is based on the design of the light. The section provides overall reading how the daylight penetrates "in-between" space and is also reflected by the angled surfaces of the building reaching

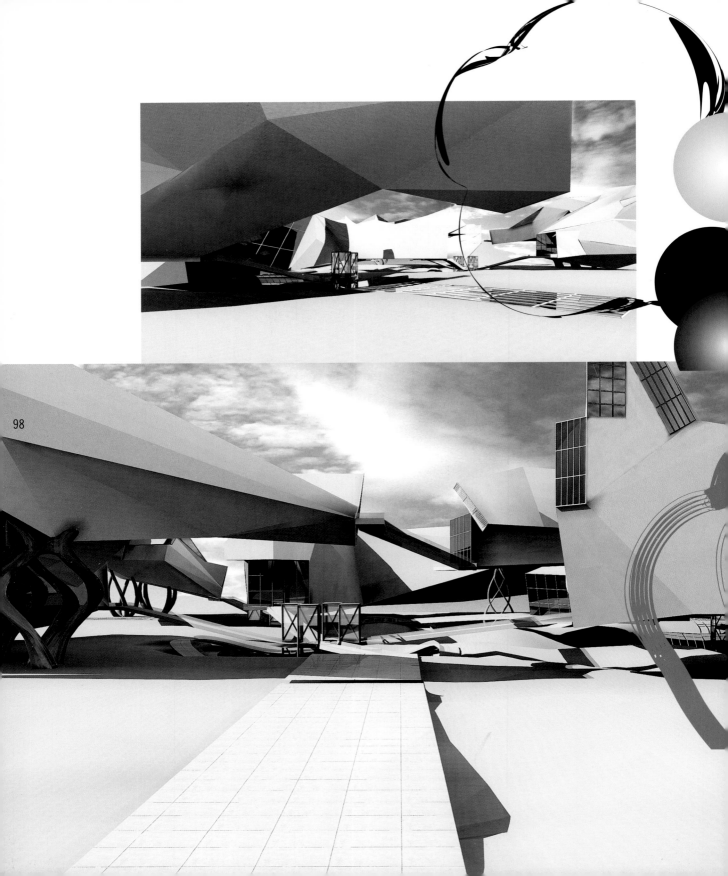

even the deepest parts of the facilities under the landscape.

Placing the various facilities underground enables good climatic conditions for the spaces, which are provided with light, but also protected from overheating through the connection ramps, which act as a brise-soiliers.

The main surface itself (our new landscape) is divided into six main areas (theme park, equipped park, dunal park, open air exhibition, Nile park, and extension area for further public spaces), connected through link systems and five main connection nodes.

Through the five main nodes, connecting ramps, und gangways under the surface it is possible to build the network of infrastructure, which can be also read as a hyper-textual organization.

The actual building, above the landscape, provides more than just the exhibited items in a different way. It embodies the concept of the "house of life" with mixed use (permanent collections, temporary exhibitions, special exhibitions, conservation laboratories, etc). The visitor can be part of the scientific and research work.

Even with the expressional formal language of the building, common materials will be used, such as reinforced concrete, steel construction and regular curtain wall facades, as well as local materials for the pavements and floors.

As structural element we are applying an "organic structure". This is based on using properties of skeletal structures to solve geometrical problems of bearing weight and absorbing stress for buildings.

Main connection node

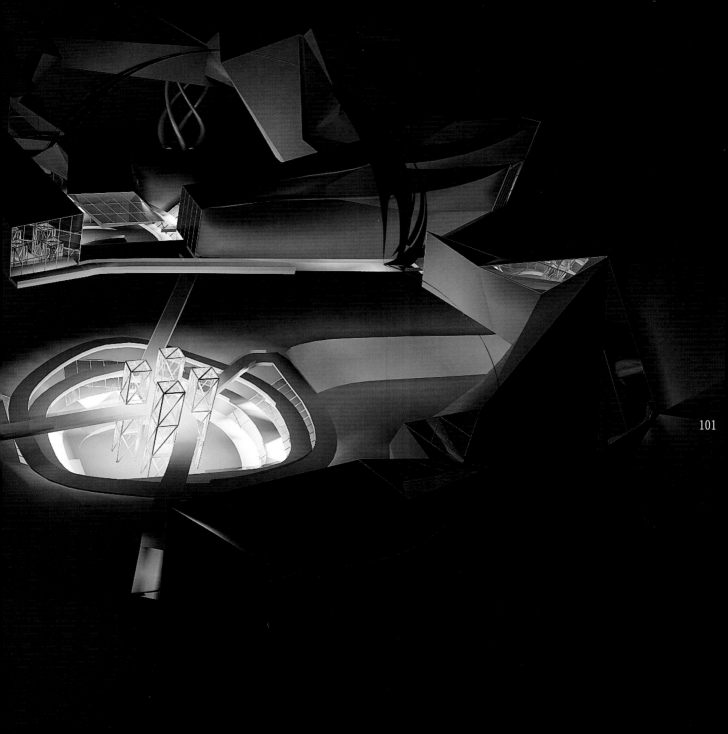

Museum concept:

The museum is conceived as an interior city with many routes. The visitors can follow pre-defined paths, but they can also choose their own route and explore the museum in their very own individual way with no fixed beginning, middle or end, but rather as multiple sequences that can be accessed or departed from at many points. The spaces are sequences with certain themes and have settings, which can be changed and modified at any time, supported by multimedia means. The exhibition spaces are in most cases columnless interiors and have generic form, which allows free organization by museum's curator and even split-levels.

The spaces are not conceived as a "Wunderkammer" for many objects, but as a new museum concept: "Network of Experience and Knowledge", as our main motive.

Diverse settings are also enhanced by multimedia installations, for example: "Virtual Light, Virtual Water (as important elements for Egyptian civilization) - terminals where children can virtually and interactively build the

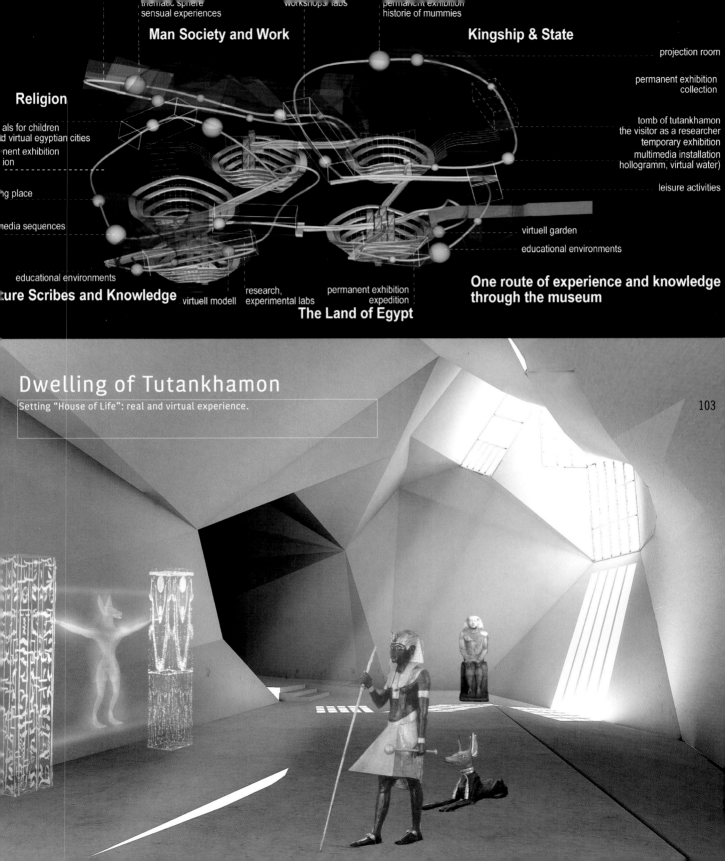

Man Society and Work

thematic sphere
sensual experiences

workshops/labs

permanent exhibition
historie of mummies

Kingship & State

projection room

permanent exhibition
collection

Religion

als for children
d virtual egyptian cities
nent exhibition
ion

g place

media sequences

tomb of tutankhamon
the visitor as a researcher
temporary exhibition
multimedia installation
hollogramm, virtual water)

leisure activities

virtuell garden
educational environments

educational environments
ure Scribes and Knowledge

virtuell modell

research,
experimental labs

permanent exhibition
expedition

The Land of Egypt

One route of experience and knowledge
through the museum

Dwelling of Tutankhamon

Setting "House of Life": real and virtual experience.

104

Entrance to the royal tomb

old Egyptian cities (e.g. Memphis) from the bottom up. There are also sensual elements of space atmosphere, like sounds and even smells. The visitor is thus invited to be also a researcher.

All spaces are connected to the general computer system and its database. A.I. organizational structure and system of the museum's dynamic exhibitions is networked similarly to the real organization of the spaces. It's control can be seen as an interface between the real and the virtual. The so-called "mind maps" of this system can easily be built and transformed in other media, for example website concepts for the Internet.

The urban situation, architectural design and museum concept introduce together a model for, and approach to, the museum of the 21st century. It is our cultural message to the New Museum.

GRAZ, AUS-TRIA

the thing and the wing

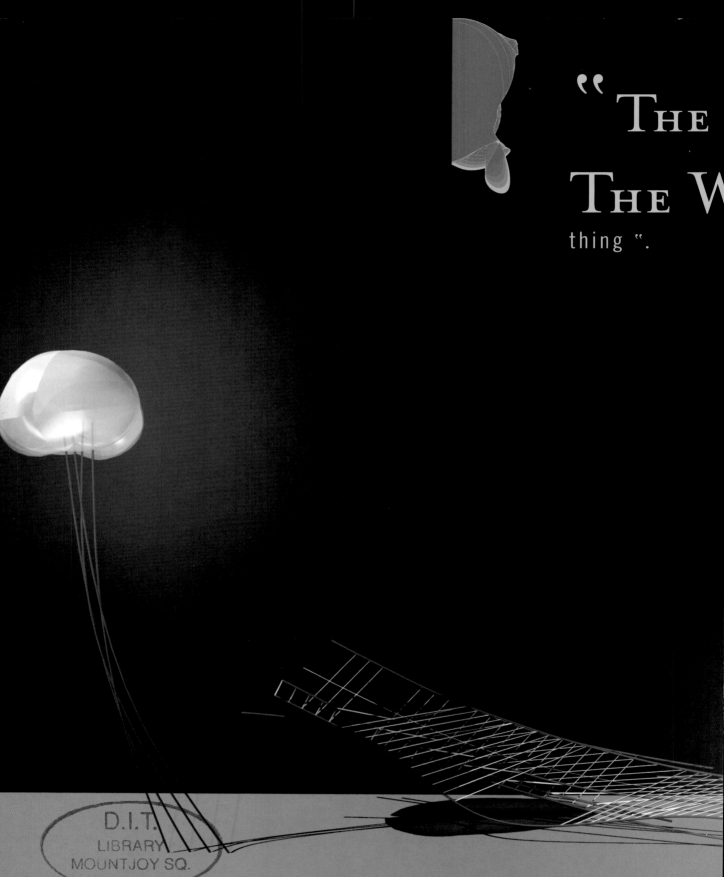

"THE

THE W

thing ".

HING AND

Soundtrack to the project " Gateway Graz 2003

NG CAN BE *everything*, THE THING AND THE WING CAN *mean* any-

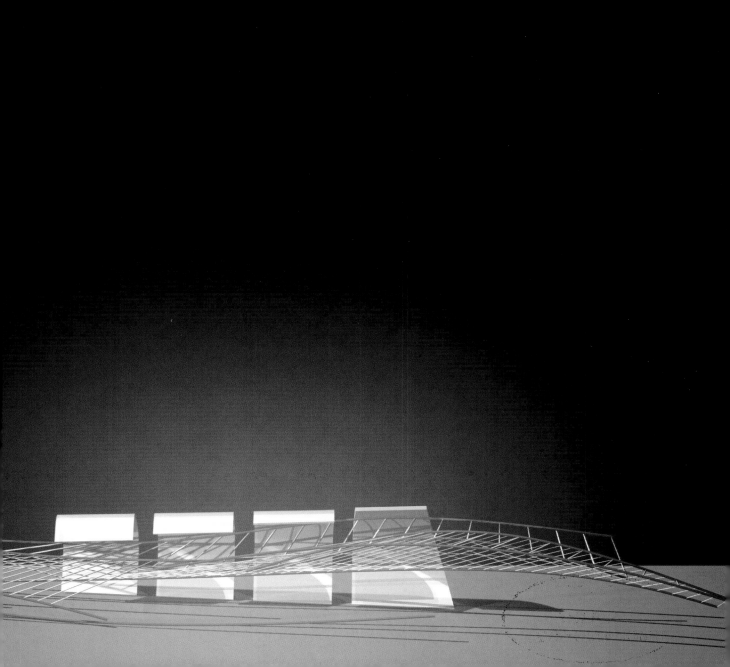

"supermodified horizin"   noise membrane   "m...ap..."

polymorpher Übergang   polymorpher Verbindungs-Körper   "deep surface"

virtueller Strömungsraum   60/6/5m   Animations-(Wind)Kanal   Partikel-Wolke

Scatter   Kraftfelder deformieren gerichtete Strömung
                 (Particelsimulation mit Kraftfeldern)

          Modify: Flows and Forces

Vertical Push   Raum-Linien (NURBS)

Computer simulations / Project development

"*THE THING AND THE WING*"

symbolizes a state of mobility, distortion and flows, a certain mood and a programmatic openness and nondogmatic definitions. Loose architecture made of steel and translucent polymorph surfaces and bodies temporarily captures one possible state of the flow simulation. Virtual view-lines are distorted and atmospheric effects are used as parameters or behaviors for simulations (*wind, noise, fluid, gas*). These interact with the actual movements of the (*car*) drivers. Consequently, the installation is not programmatically tied to the individual events of the "Cultural Capital Graz 2003", but conveys a general mood the whole year over - an exciting atmosphere. The Wing consists of several layers and is an information carrier, an aerodynamic structure, which you pass and due to the velocity perceive only abstractly. The Thing is an object you perceive from the distance and approach over a longer period of time — regarded symbolically, a relationship comparable to the one between the Herrengasse (*facade*) and the Uhrturm (*vertical symbol*) in Graz, for example. The two sculptures, horizontal and vertical, are linked together conceptually, forming a unit (*merging through speed*) only through the perception of the drivers (*spatial lengthening*). The two elements describe no locality but instead a movement in time and are dislocated. Directly along the highway, in close proximity to the airport, they act as dynamic vectors. The traffic concept stands for the circulation of ideas and theories. The motion is not to be understood merely as a function, you realize it as an inner experience. The charm of this infrastructural thinking lies in its premise that subjectivity discards the final explanation and takes the object as departure point. 109

The Thing

Schnitt 1

SCHNIT

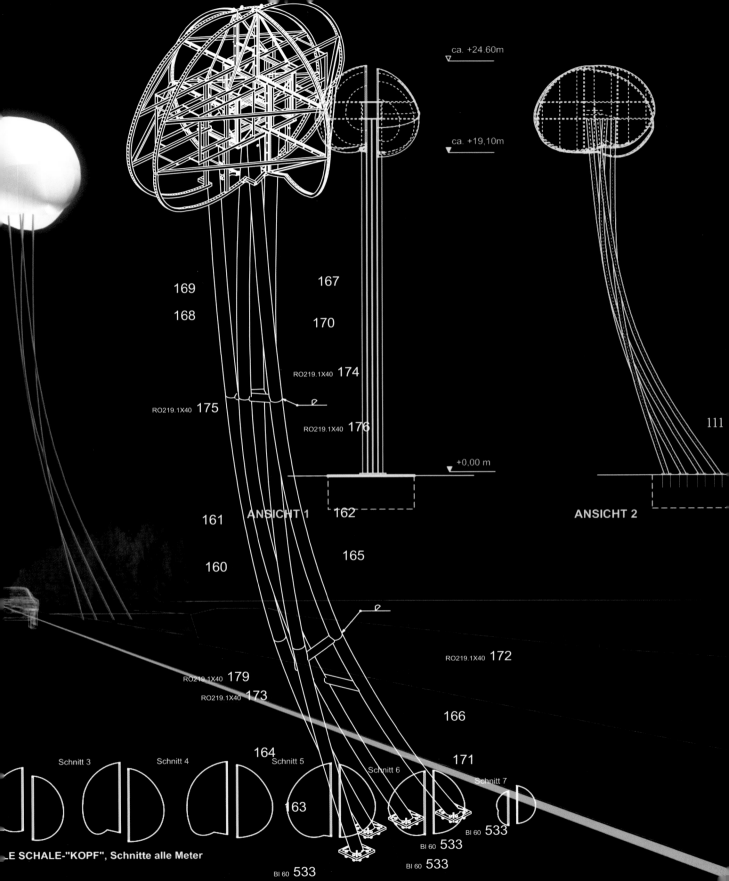

ca. +24.60m

ca. +19,10m

169

168

167

170

RO219.1X40 174

RO219.1X40 175

RO219.1X40 176

+0,00 m

111

ANSICHT 1

162

ANSICHT 2

161

165

160

RO219.1X40 172

RO219.1X40 179

RO219.1X40 173

166

Schnitt 3

Schnitt 4

164

Schnitt 5

171

Schnitt 6

Schnitt 7

163

Bl 60 533

LE SCHALE-"KOPF", Schnitte alle Meter

Bl 60 533

Bl 60 533

Bl 60 533

Bl 60 533

THE WI

ca. +9,30 m

WL-5
WL-1
WL-3
WL-4

+0,00 m

ANSICHT "THE WING"

"WÄNDE":
Fiberglas, 4-lagig (4mm)
mit seitl. Rahmen aus HEB140-Profilen

PERSPEKTIVE "THE WING"

WL-7
WL-9
WL-8
WL-11
WL-10

116

The Thing and The Wing it can be a thing
The Thing and The Wing can mean anything
I am driving on the road from nowhere
No one can tell me where it is gonna lead me
But to come back you have to go away
No one knows what is gonna happen

wing

The Thing at the
seaside

We believe that every architectural project *needs its own Soundtrack as well*. Together with the five young musicians and DJs we created and produced the CD containing 5 "the Thing and the Wing" songs.
The main idea was to take the concept of the installation and transport it with the other medium then visual. The sound expands the architectural project for a new quality, since the audio track, similar to the film music, increase the atmosphere and brings the new associative imagination. The rhythm of the music follows the object. It flows through the samples, never stopping; as on the freeway there is no standstill.
Mixing various medias is typical for ORTLOS way of working and it can be seen as an experiment, to initiate and develop new methods of collaborative work.

SONGS

Music CD

THE THING AND THE WING
IT CAN BE EVERYTHING
THE THING AND
THE WING CAN
ANYTHING

The Thing and The Wing it can be

everything

I AM DRIVING ON THE
The Thing and The Wing can mean anything
ROAD FROM NOWHERE
NO ONE CAN TELL
ME WHERE IT IS
I am driving on the road from nowhere
GONNA LEAD ME
No one can tell me where it is gonna lead me
BUT TO COME BACK YOU
HAVE TO GO AWAY
But to come back you have to go away
NO ONE KNOWS WHAT
No one knows what is gonna happen
IS GONNA HAPPEN

124

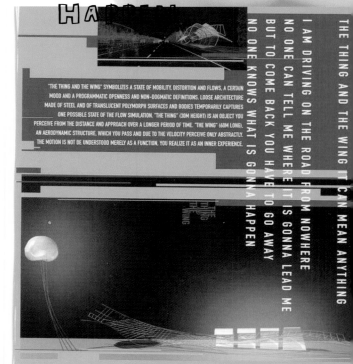

"THE THING AND THE WING" SYMBOLIZES A STATE OF MOBILITY, DISTORTION AND FLOWS, A CERTAIN
MOOD AND A PROGRAMMATIC OPENNESS AND NON-DOGMATIC DEFINITIONS. LOOSE ARCHITECTURE
MADE OF STEEL AND OF TRANSLUCENT POLYMORPH SURFACES AND BODIES TEMPORARILY CAPTURES
ONE POSSIBLE STATE OF THE FLOW SIMULATION. "THE THING" (30M HEIGHT) IS AN OBJECT YOU
PERCEIVE FROM THE DISTANCE AND APPROACH OVER A LONGER PERIOD OF TIME. "THE WING" (60M LONG),
AN AERODYNAMIC STRUCTURE, WHICH YOU PASS AND DUE TO THE VELOCITY PERCEIVE ONLY ABSTRACTLY.
THE MOTION IS NOT BE UNDERSTOOD MERELY AS A FUNCTION, YOU REALIZE IT AS AN INNER EXPERIENCE.

THE THING AND THE WING IT CAN MEAN ANYTHING
I AM DRIVING ON THE ROAD FROM NOWHERE
NO ONE CAN TELL ME WHERE IT IS GONNA LEAD ME
BUT TO COME BACK YOU HAVE TO GO AWAY
NO ONE KNOWS WHAT IS GONNA HAPPEN

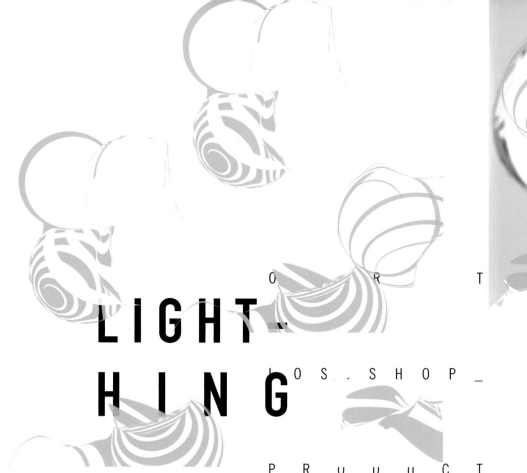

LIGHT_

HING

O   R   T

OS.SHOP _

PRODUCT

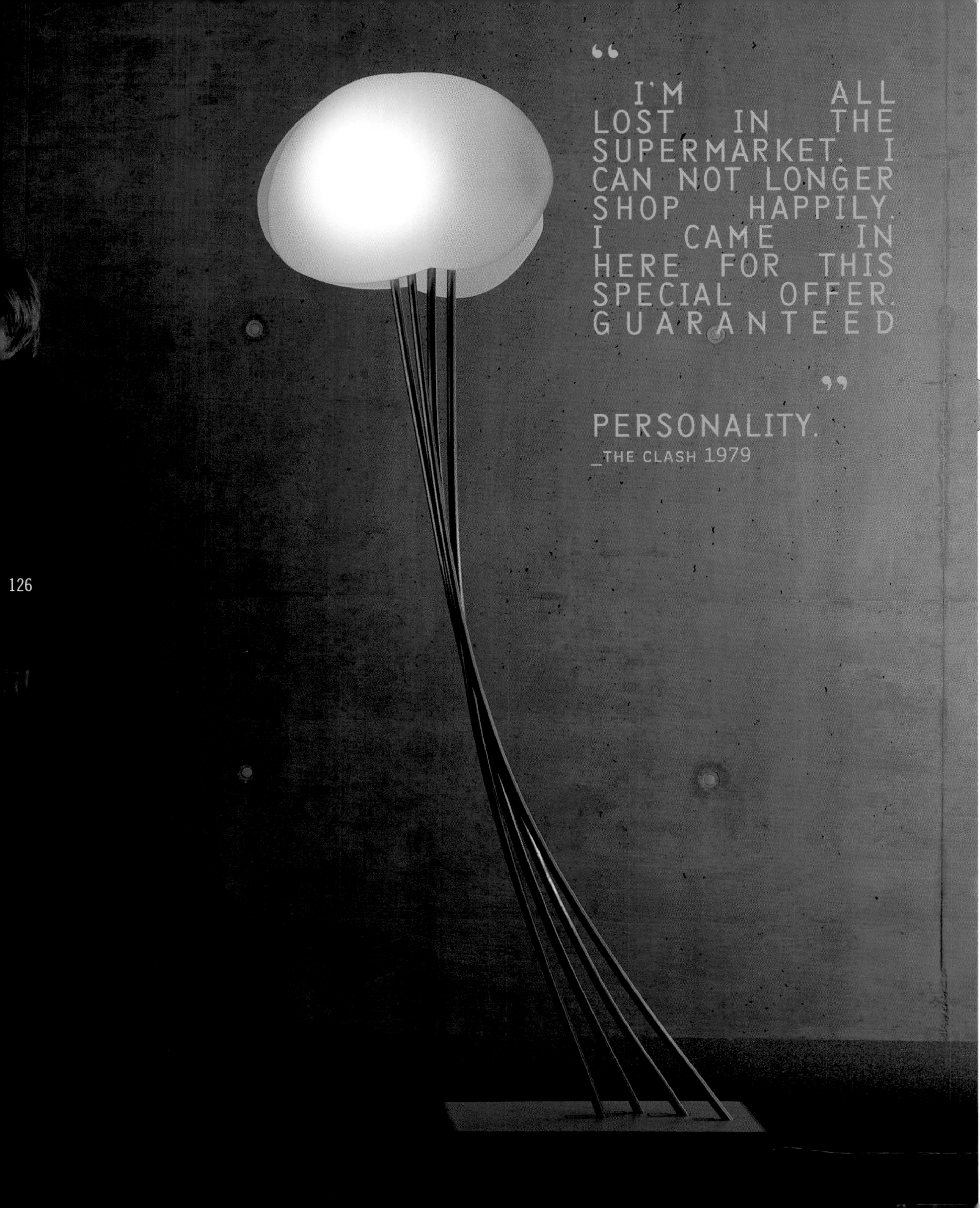

"
I'M ALL
LOST IN THE
SUPERMARKET. I
CAN NOT LONGER
SHOP HAPPILY.
I CAME IN
HERE FOR THIS
SPECIAL OFFER.
GUARANTEED
"

PERSONALITY.
_THE CLASH 1979

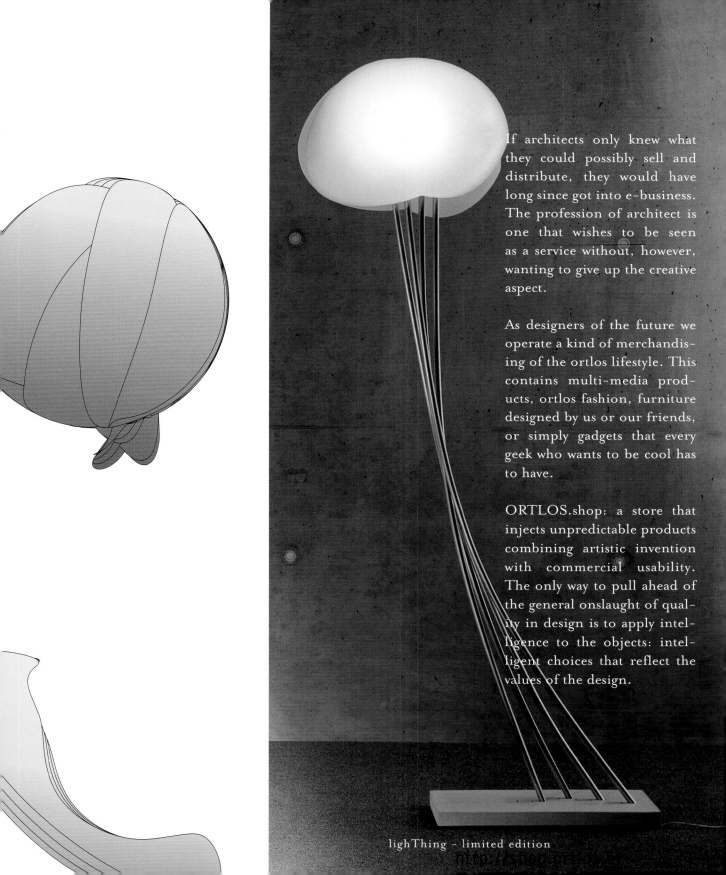

If architects only knew what they could possibly sell and distribute, they would have long since got into e-business. The profession of architect is one that wishes to be seen as a service without, however, wanting to give up the creative aspect.

As designers of the future we operate a kind of merchandising of the ortlos lifestyle. This contains multi-media products, ortlos fashion, furniture designed by us or our friends, or simply gadgets that every geek who wants to be cool has to have.

ORTLOS.shop: a store that injects unpredictable products combining artistic invention with commercial usability. The only way to pull ahead of the general onslaught of quality in design is to apply intelligence to the objects: intelligent choices that reflect the values of the design.

ligThing - limited edition

He, she and the thing

130

LEUCHTKÖRPER: ABMASSE: BOUNDING BOX ~ 600X535X430 MATERIAL: PMMA-XT POLYMER 3 MM OBERFLÄCHE: OPAL SATINIERT HERSTELLUNGSPROZESS: VAKUUM-TIEFZIEHVERFAHREN TECHNIKBOX: ABMASSE: 296X80X84 MATERIAL: ALU-BLECH 2MM FUNKTIONEN: INTEGRIERT - STEUERELEKTRONIK, LAMPENFASSUNGEN FÜR 4X60W GLÜHBIRNEN; APLIZIERT - HALTERUNGEN FÜR DIE SEITLICH AUFKLAPPBAREN LAMPENSCHIRME FÜSSE: MATERIAL: NIROROHR D=17MM OBERFLÄCHE: MATT SOCKEL: ABMASSE: 300X500X35 MATERIAL: FEIN-BETON OBERFLÄCHE: STIRNFLÄCHEN UND 8MM RAND DER OBERSEITE SANDGESTRAHLT, FARBLOS LACKIERT GESAMT: GEWICHT 23,5KG HÖHE 203CM - VERSCHIEDENFARBIGE LEUCHTMITTEL IM LIEFERUMFANG ENTHALTEN

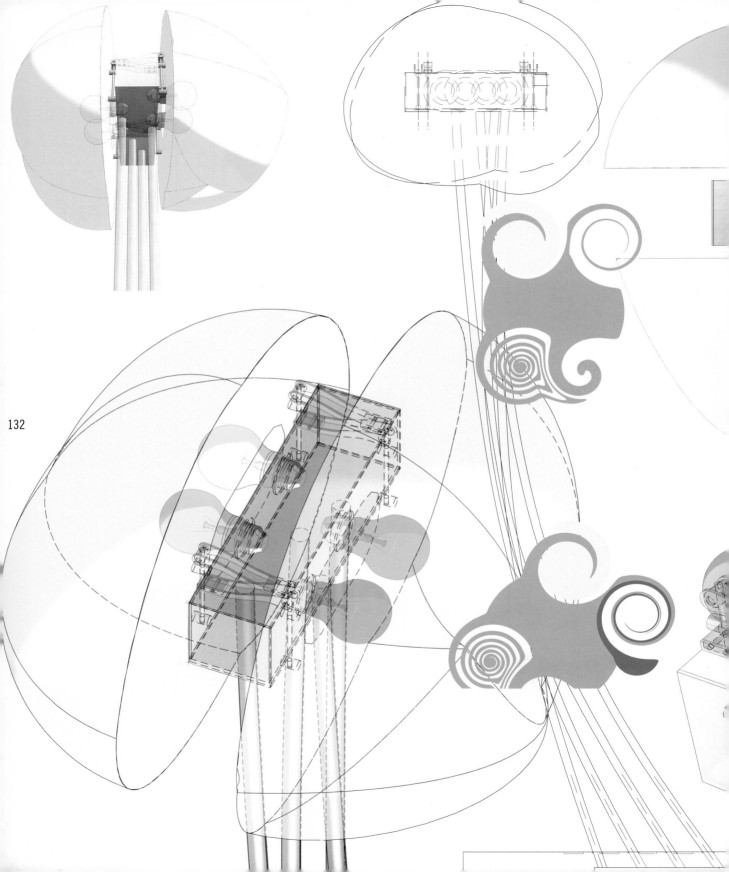

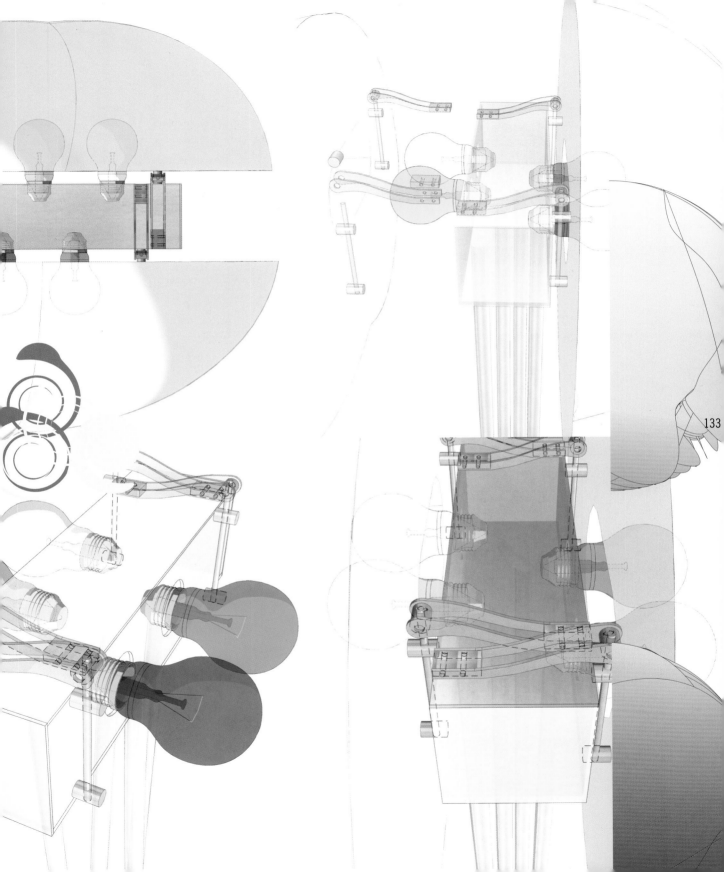

FIELDS OF THINGS

Why everything becomes a wrapping / a cover / a cloth / fashioning the year 2000 / representation & high aspirations

Graz, Austria.
cultural spheres / cultural context

KUNSTHAUS

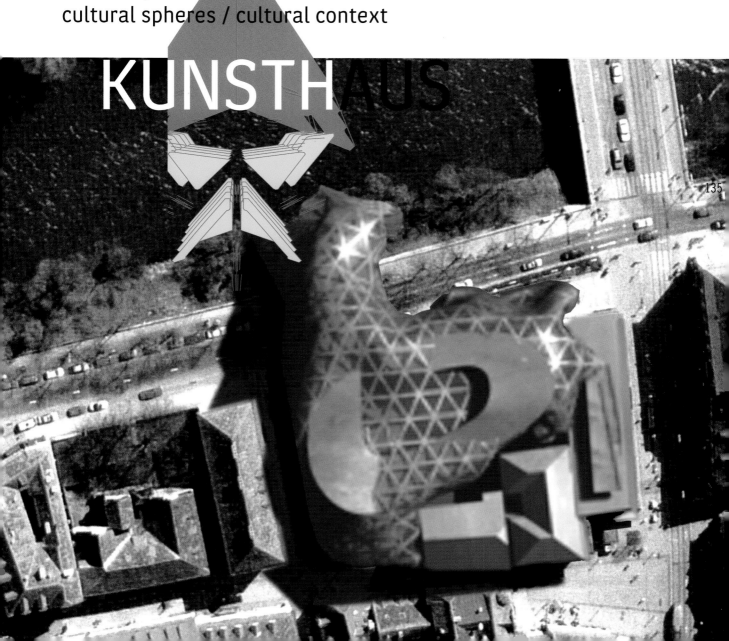

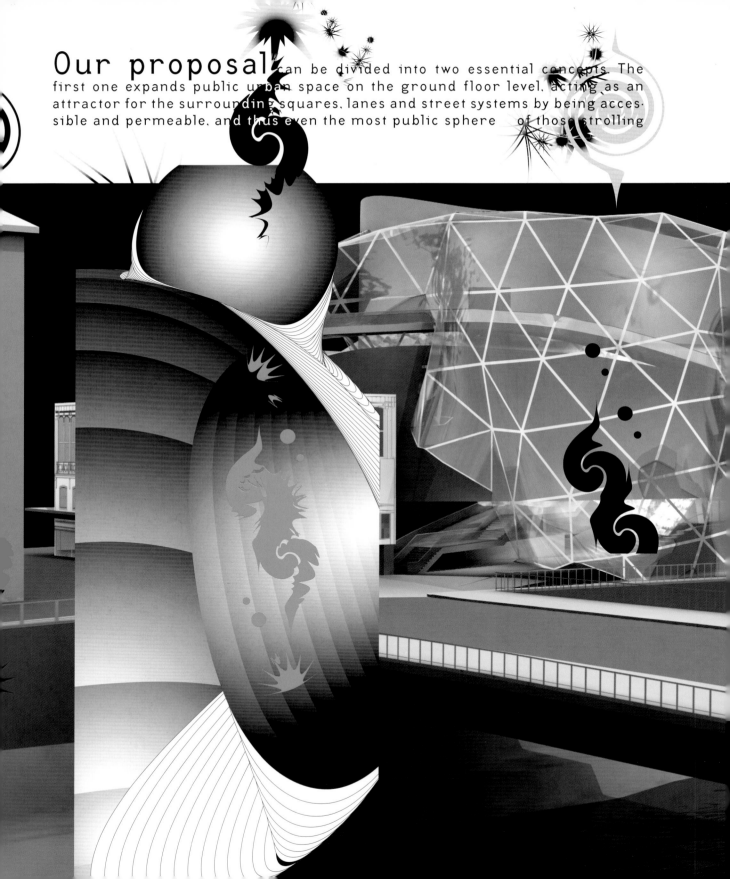

Our proposal can be divided into two essential concepts. The first one expands public urban space on the ground floor level, acting as an attractor for the surrounding squares, lanes and street systems by being accessible and permeable, and thus even the most public sphere of those strolling

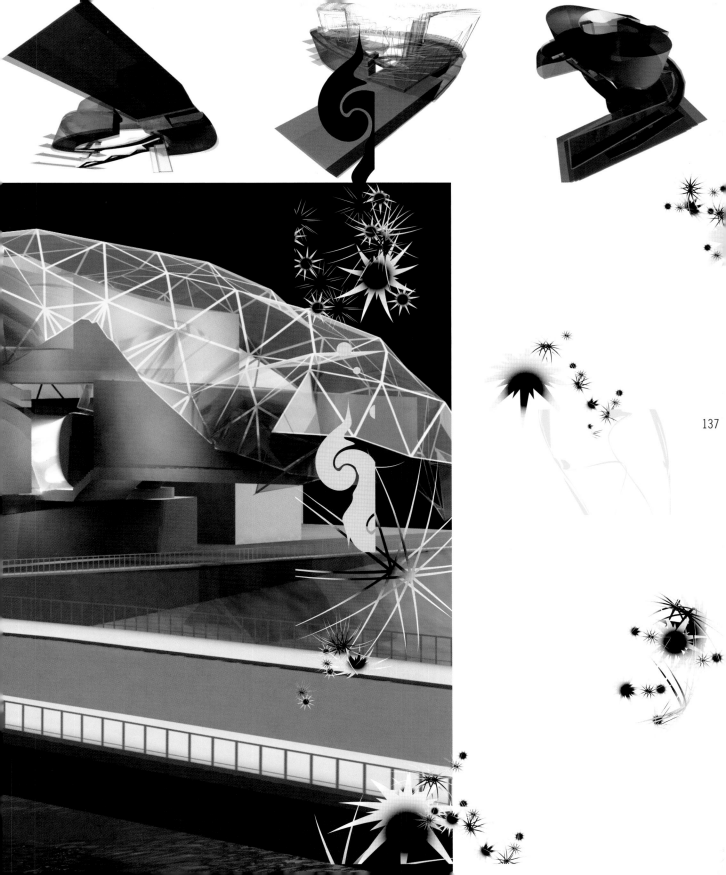

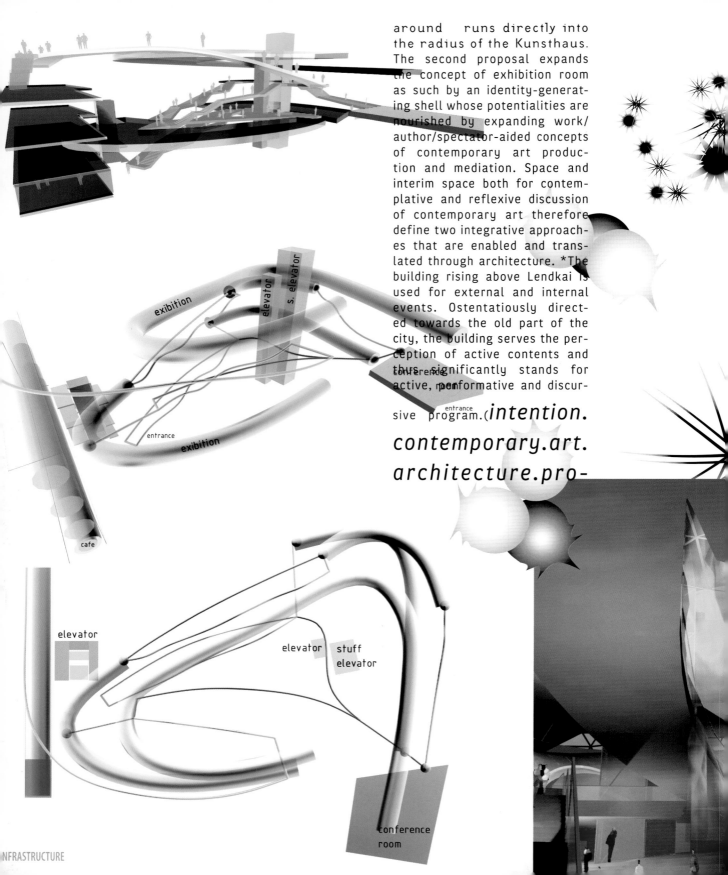

around runs directly into the radius of the Kunsthaus. The second proposal expands the concept of exhibition room as such by an identity-generating shell whose potentialities are nourished by expanding work/author/spectator-aided concepts of contemporary art production and mediation. Space and interim space both for contemplative and reflexive discussion of contemporary art therefore define two integrative approaches that are enabled and translated through architecture. *The building rising above Lendkai is used for external and internal events. Ostentatiously directed towards the old part of the city, the building serves the perception of active contents and thus significantly stands for active, performative and discursive program.(*intention.*

contemporary.art.

architecture.pro-

exibition

elevator

s. elevator

entrance

exibition

conference

entrance

cafe

elevator

elevator

stuff
elevator

conference
room

cess).

Our draft starts from social processes which, going beyond institutionalized public mechanisms, are in a position to generate identification and meaning. In this sense, the space reserved for the exhibition of works of art is a fixed local (socio-political) determinant; a transcended physical expression whose demands, claims and wishes can be translated in a simple three-dimensional way. Beyond this consensual context of an exhibition space for art, there is a space which gains importance (and a social sphere) only when actively embedded in the aspects of the programmatic, social and communicative – a process which cannot be curated. Intervention makes possible the experience, use and appropriation of these envisaged spatial qualities.

In the context of Graz we anticipate an active pool in all artistic fields. A situation that we would not sufficiently do justice to with the classical social infrastructures (that naturally serve those on the receiving end). Our concept offers interim zones which represent one of the most crucial resources for the production of art at the present moment and which account for the fact that art production over the last few years has been characterized by de-institutionalized, artistic and social practices. Away from a movement from the center into the periphery. If art production changes, or rather the applied practices of the artists, then this interim zone will be in the position to offer an action radius for intervention. In this way we dissolve function for the benefit of non-determination (new media, education and youth) while knowing precisely about the essential meaning of these areas and their future potential.

ORGANIZATIO
NAL PRINCIPLE

139

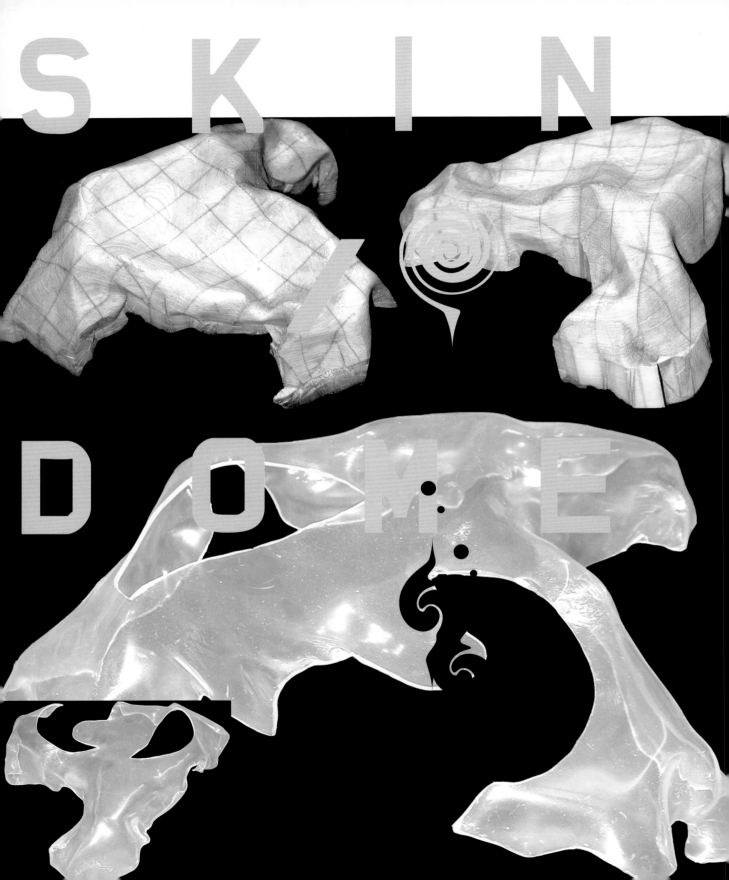

SKIN / DOME

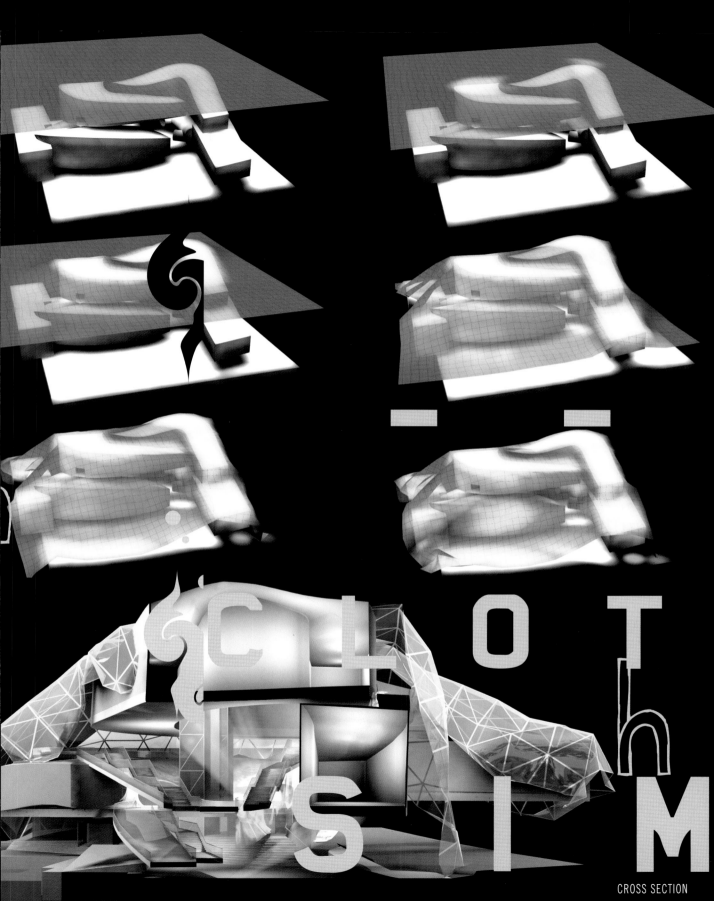

CROSS SECTION

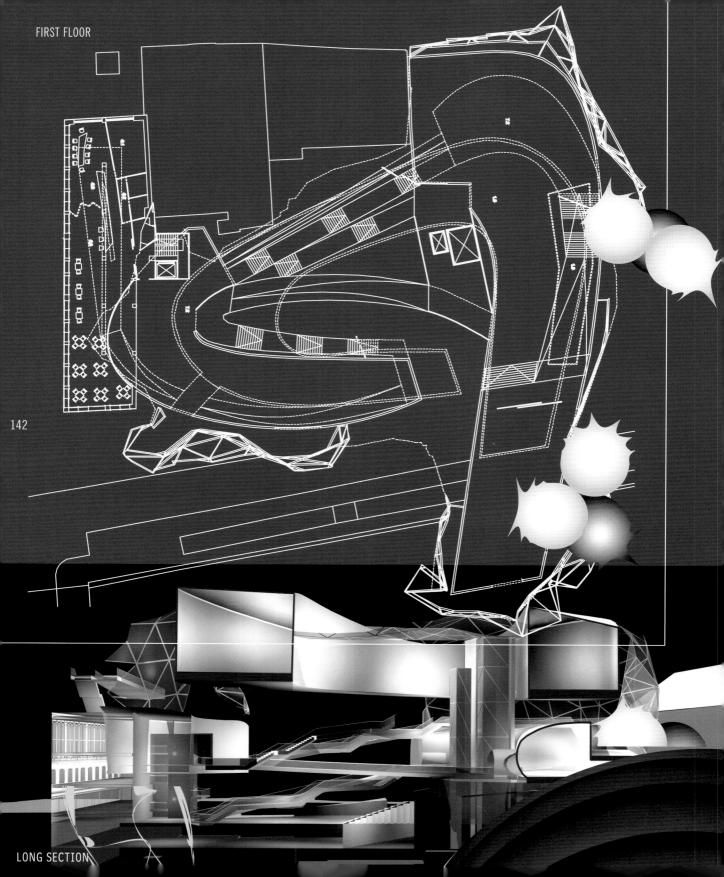

FIRST FLOOR

142

LONG SECTION

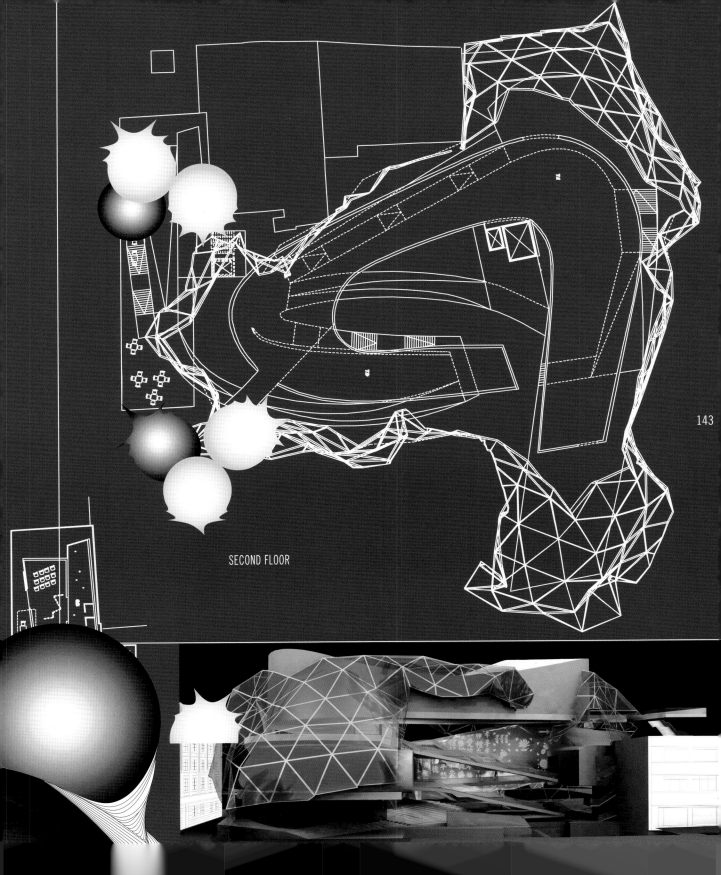

SECOND FLOOR

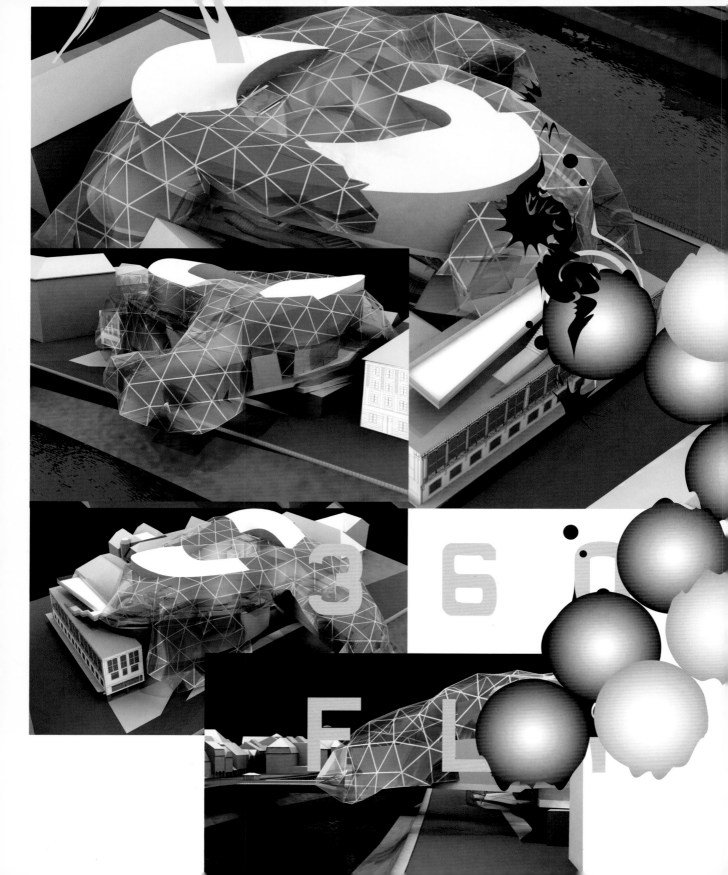

· art does not end at its limits, but that it is an activity that has an impact on life, and that it is similar to an operation. When we continue to think about art and artistic practice, the international discourse leads us away from the idea of a specialized and autonomous field towards cultural production on the one hand and social practice on the other hand. The new term of cultural production by artists means interdisciplinary analyses of art in a social field, reaching beyond their specific institutions and practices. It is about a space of "artistic practice" or one that mediates this practice in the contemporary sense.

NETWORK OF THE ART OPERATIONS

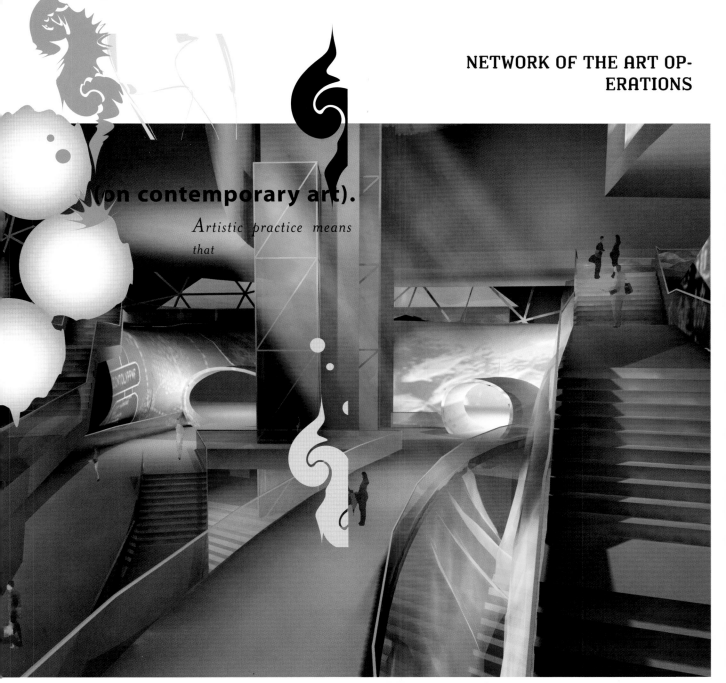

(on contemporary art).

Artistic practice means that

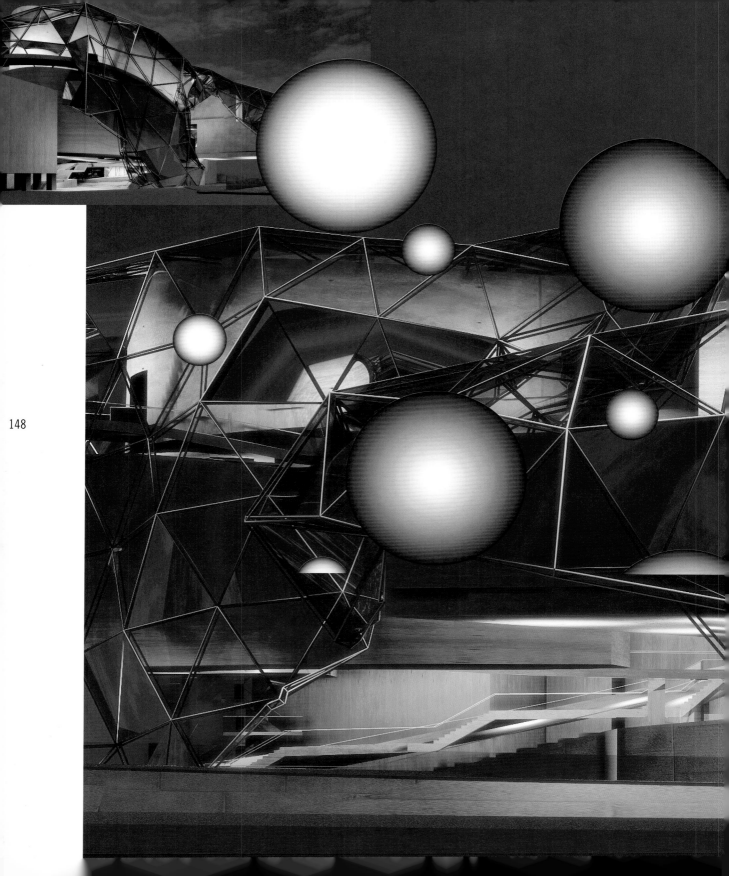

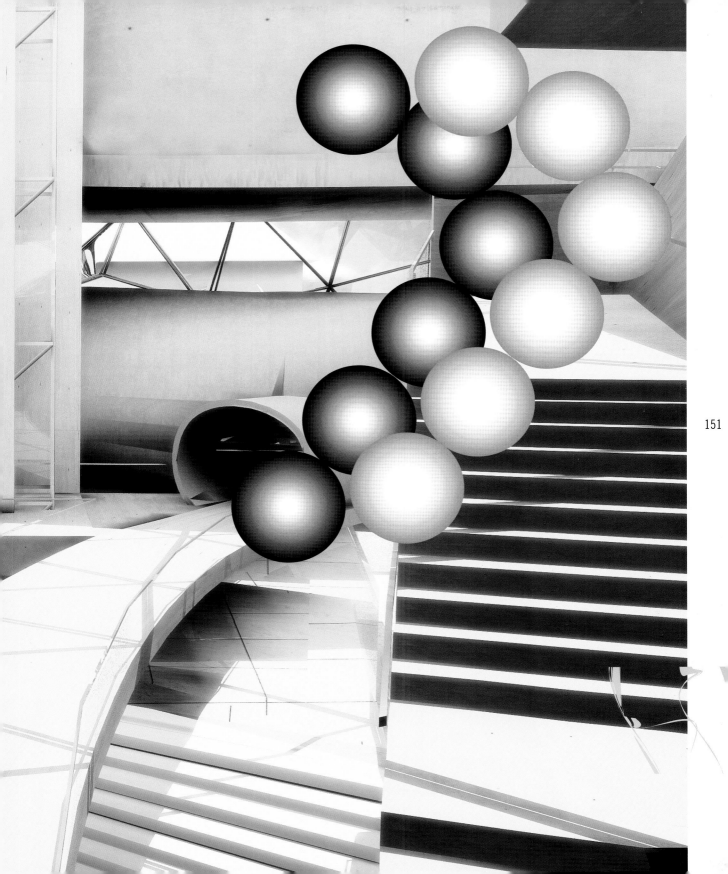

Urban Park
La Paz, Bolivia

URBAN

DESIGN

FEATURING GUENTHER

BRUS

A green grove is the poetic offer of an enchanting new site design for the city of La Paz. The main idea is to incorporate the Urban Park of La Paz into a natural network, through defining its own identity.

The orientation towards the city's ecological improvement demands an urban design concept that offers clean water features, new links to the neighborhoods and safe recreational facilities in an informal way.
- New access points and many connecting paths and walks offer linkage within the grid of the city.
- The green squares close to the site include information points that give prior program information for tourists as well as for the people of La Paz.

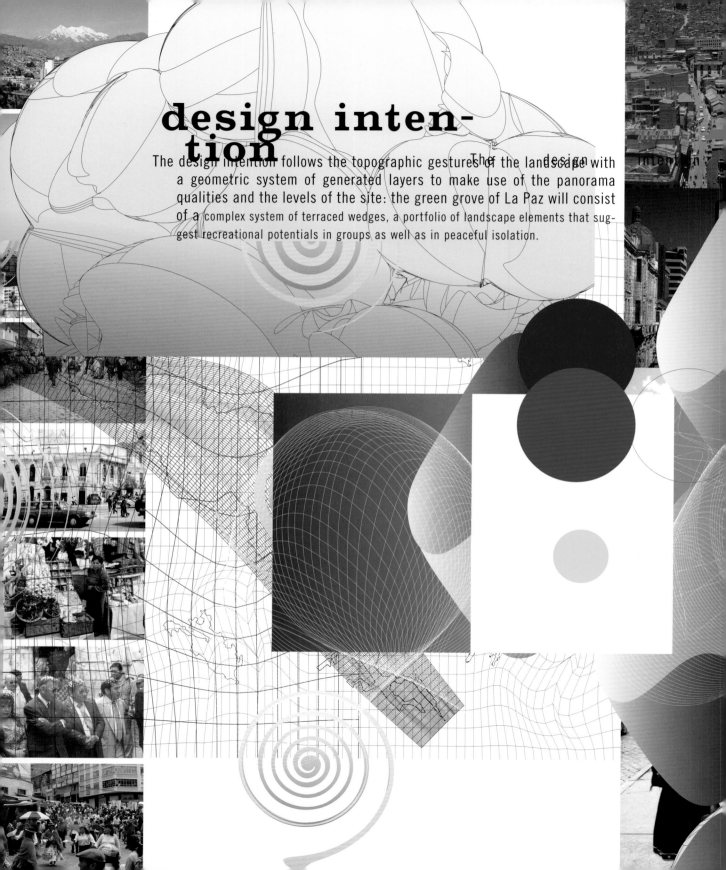

design inten-
tion

The design intention follows the topographic gestures of the landscape with a geometric system of generated layers to make use of the panorama qualities and the levels of the site: the green grove of La Paz will consist of a complex system of terraced wedges, a portfolio of landscape elements that suggest recreational potentials in groups as well as in peaceful isolation.

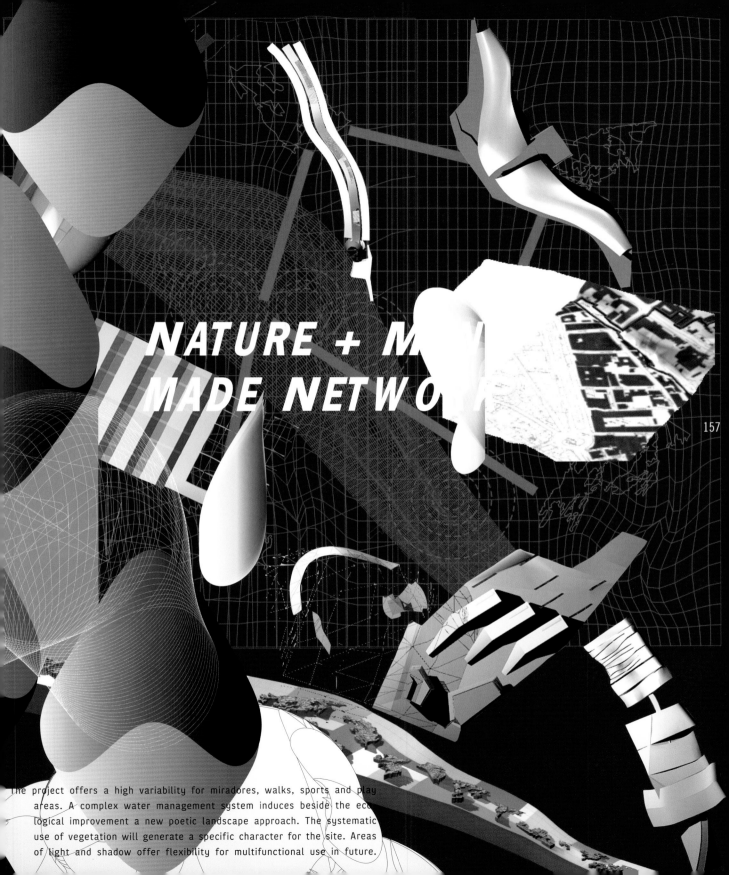

NATURE + MAN MADE NETWORK

The project offers a high variability for miradores, walks, sports and play areas. A complex water management system induces beside the ecological improvement a new poetic landscape approach. The systematic use of vegetation will generate a specific character for the site. Areas of light and shadow offer flexibility for multifunctional use in future.

EN CADA ABISMO VIVE
LA DIOSA DEL

CIO, SIEMPRE QUE NO SEA PERTUR-
BADA.

The departure point for the design is a system of 4 schematic diagrams or layers which can be superimposed.

Layer: Topography Flow – Based on the topographical elements found on the site: the river (reshaped and newly developed), La Poeta Avenue (as infrastructural backbone and tangential access to the park), and remarkable landscape. This layer considers the park as a dynamic structure where each element follows the vectoral flow. It also brings up the architectural intention to incorporate the landscape in a new vocabulary.

Layer: Program Network – With given program to be fulfilled and distributed in a more dispersed manner. It deals with different qualities of the whole site, rather than concentration and production of the areas of high density. Beside the build content there are programmed surfaces in terms of zoning the park based on activities and events, and avoiding the classical relationships between paths and fields. This also supports the idea of future unforeseen uses. The third element is the vegetation space, which can be defined through different types of trees and bushes producing the most fantastic spatial configurations.

Layer: Poetic Texts – This is an abstract layer based on 12 sentences which are the main connectors or inspirations for the formal expressions. They build the sequences of sections for the open story of the park. The story has no beginning and no ending, it is readable from any point and any direction. This means that the visitors can experience the park always in a new manner depending on the route of exploration they may choose. This layer also

filters the information flows.
Layer: Data matrix – A layer coming from somewhere else and projected onto the site. It basically consists of interpretated information, a matrix of the parametric computer simulations of the processes not connected to local conditions. It deals with the global topics affecting every part of the worldwide community. It also opens up new possibilities and provides opportunities for development on its own strength.

MA**S**TERPLAN

arts & crafts
information center
forum for young people
& congress center
memory & future
science & technology
art & contemporary culture

161

EL FIRMAMENTO SOBRE BOLIVIA ES EL FIEL REFLEJO
DE UN CONDOR AZUL CELESTE.

das firmament über bo-
livien gleicht einem himmelblauen
kondor

EL RÍO ES LA ARTERIA EN EL CORAZÓN DE LA CIU-
DAD.

in fluss ist die blutbahn im herzen einer stadt.

LA PAZ ES UN PUERTO EN EL MAR DEL FIRMAMEN-
TO.

a paz ist eine hafenstadt am meer des firmaments.

EN CADA ABISMO VIVE LA DIOSA DEL SILENCIO, SIEM-
PRE QUE NO SEA PERTURBADA.

in jeder schlucht haust die göttin der stille, wenn sie nicht
gestört wird.

EN ESTOS TIEMPOS, EL SOL DE LOS QUECHUA Y DE
LOS AYMARA GIRA ALREDEDOR DE GALAXIAS

die sonne der quechuas und aymaras dreht sich heute um un-
bekannte galaxien.

LA LUNA LLENA ENCIMA DE LA CORDILLERA REAL ES
DE ESTAÑO Y DISNEA.

der vollmond über der cordillera real ist aus zinn und atem-
not.

CASCADAS DE CAMINOS ERRADOS CAEN AL ABISMO DE
LA POESÍA.

kaskaden aus irrwegen stürzen hinab in den abgrund der
poesie.

A AQUELLOS POETAS QUE SE TROPIEZAN CONTRA LAS
YARETAS LOS CRÍTICOS LES VENDEN COMO COMBUSTI-
BLE.

dichter, die über yaretas stolpern, werden als brennstoff
von kritikern verkauft.

SOBRE EL LAGO TITICACA REPOSA EL FULGOR DEL AR-
GENTO ROBADO.

über dem titicacasee schwebt der glimmer des geraubten
silbers.

EL AMAZONAS Y EL PARANÁ REHUYEN PARA NO MOLES-
TAR CON SUS PIRAÑAS AL ALTIPLANO.

der amazonas und der parana ziehen von dannen, um den
altiplano nicht durch pirhanhas zu stören.

LA PAZ SUPERA EL MURO SÓNICO ENTRE LA GRAVEDAD Y
LA LUZ.

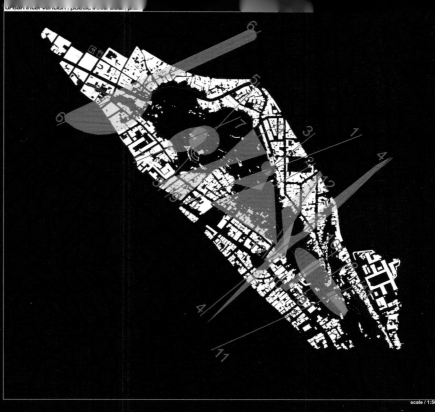

urban intervention : poetic in... ... ...

scale / 1 : 5000

Layer: Poetic Texts

— This is an abstract layer based on 12 sentences which are the main connectors or inspirations for the formal expressions. They build the sequences of sections for the open story of the park. The story has no beginning and no ending, it is readable from any point and any direction. This means that the visitors can experience the park always in a new manner depending on the route of exploration they may choose. This layer also filters the information flows.

Layer: Data matrix

— A layer coming from somewhere else and projected onto the site. It basically consists of interpretated information, a matrix of the parametric computer simulations of the processes not connected to local conditions. It deals with the global topics affecting every part of the worldwide community. It also opens up new possibilities and provides opportunities for development on its

<< From God to Goodie
- the sentences by artists
Günther Brus

POETIC INFILTRATION

la paz durchbricht die schallmauer zwischen erdschwere und

licht.

Bolivia es un país continental, tan interior como lo es el corazón de una persona o una llama.
bolivien ist ein binnenland wie das herz in einem körper eines menschen oder in einem lama

ARTS & CRAFTS

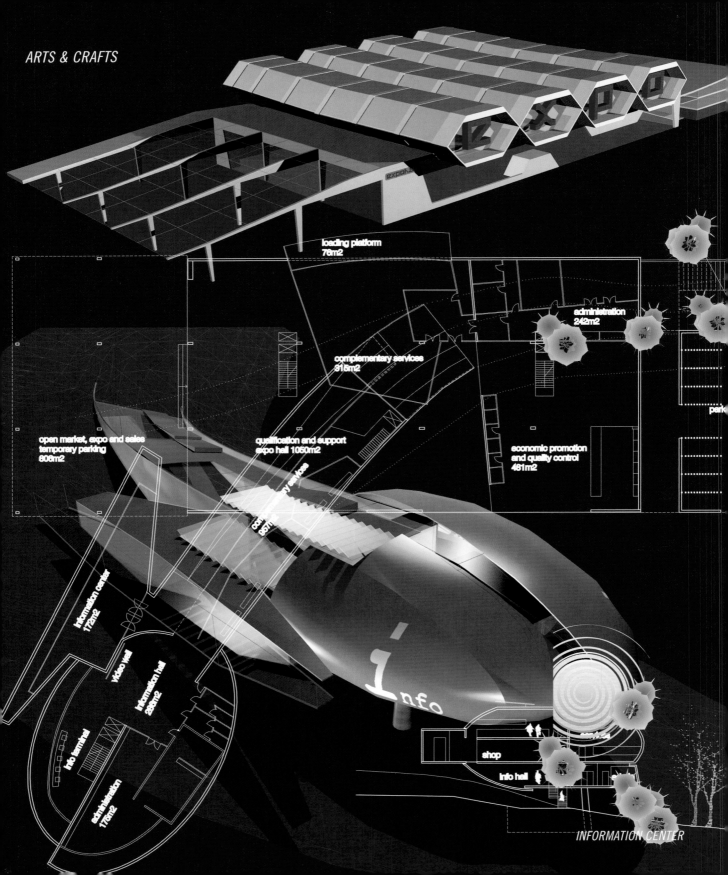

loading platform
76m2

administration
242m2

complementary services
315m2

open market, expo and sales
temporary parking
806m2

qualification and support
expo hall 1050m2

economic promotion
and quality control
481m2

complementary services
867m2

info

information center
172m2

video wall

information hall
288m2

info terminal

shop

administration
178m2

info hall

INFORMATION CENTER

ART & CONTEMPORARY CULTURE

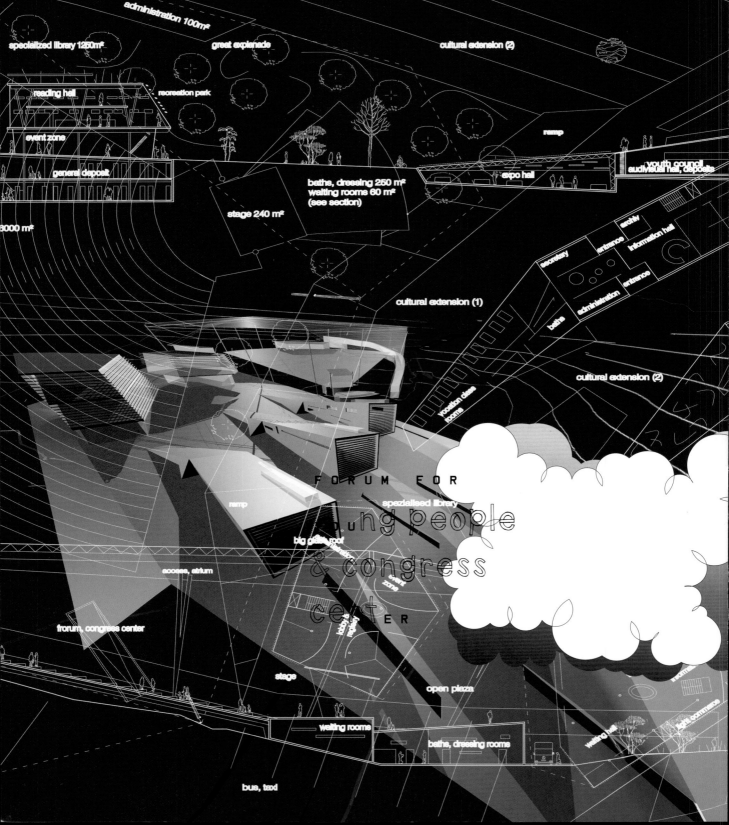

memorY AND future

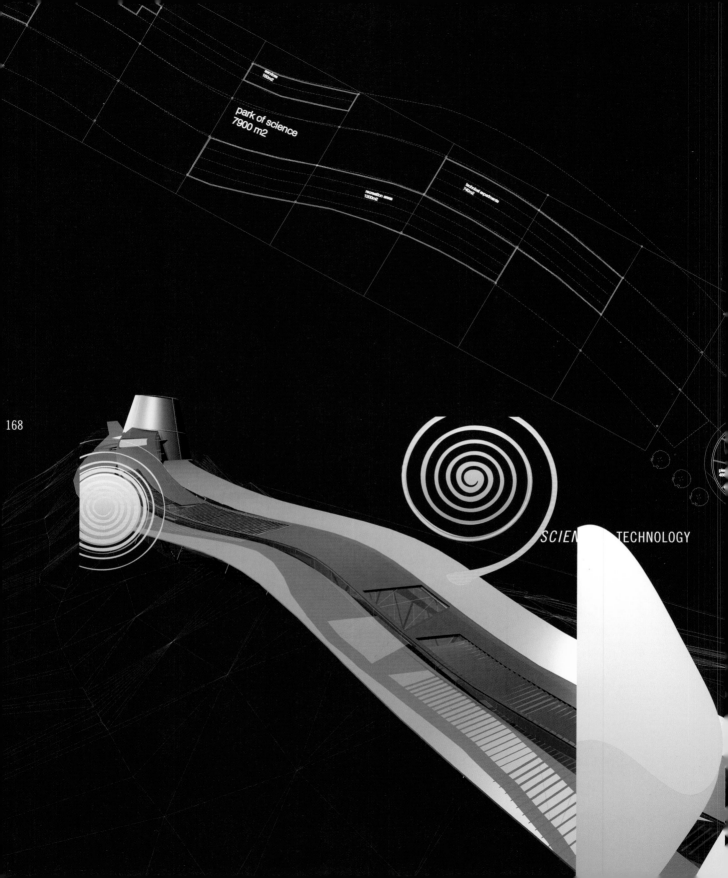

park of science
7900 m2

service
150m2

recreation areas
1200m2

technical experiments
740m2

SCIENCE TECHNOLOGY

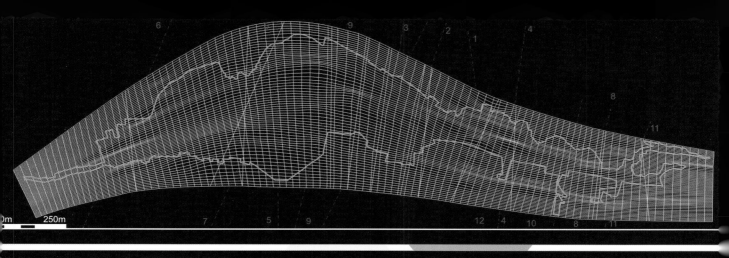

roposal . sporting & recreation fields

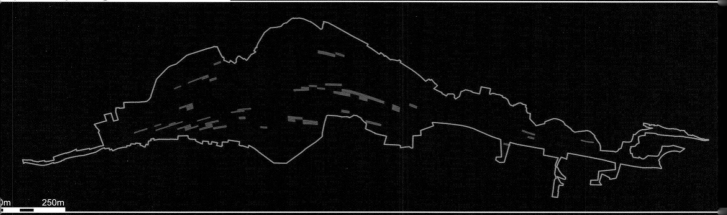

roposal . programm fields (build)

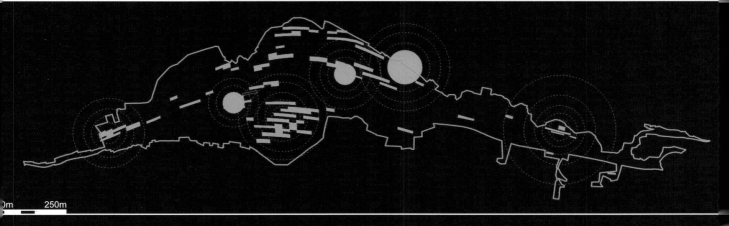

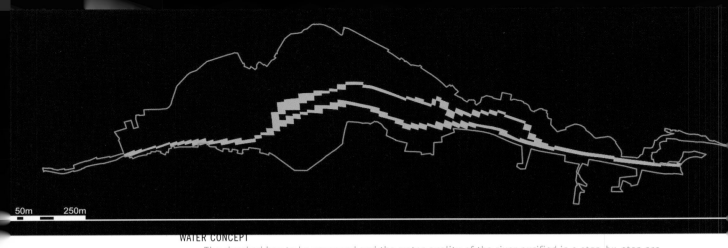

WATER CONCEPT

- The riverbed has to be reopened and the water quality of the river purified in a step-by-step process that will return ecological and hygiene quality to the neighborhood.
- A concept of river morphology demands a retention lake for heavy rain, soil stabilization and cascades for improvement of verification.
- An extra waterway will be created on the retention lake level so as to offer a chance for time-dependent drain off as well as a nice water feature with opportunities for temporary irrigation of the park areas.
- Surface water will be collected in retention basins to be used for irrigation of the planted areas.

proposal . green fields

50m   250m

PARKUSE

- Levels will be defined for miradores and for mass events
- Steep slopes will be planted with salix, eucalyptus pinus according to position of the sun

proposal . juxtaposition of the fields

50m   250m

West Kowloon Reclamation- Hong Kong

可能的未來填海區

RECLAMATION AREA

In the mid-1800's, Victoria Harbour was about 2 km wide. Back then the city was a collection of small colonial buildings. Shanty towns exploded into existence in the post WWII era due to massive inflows of refugees fleeing war and the communists. There was a huge need for scarce land, so the city became built up into the highrise haven you see today, and expanded into the harbour. Various reclamation projects at various points and especially on Hong Kong Island have narrowed the harbour quite a bit so that it is now half of what it used to be. The water is quite polluted as 1.5 million litres of raw sewage are poured into it daily.

VOXELS

The picture

on your computer screen is built up by small squares called pixels, an abbreviation of picture elements. Voxels are three-dimensional pixels (volume elements) – small rectangular blocks. In the same way as pixels are good at storing data that can be broken up into small squares, voxels are good at storing data that can be broken up into small rectangular blocks. In the same way as pixels may be stored in a two dimensional array, voxels can be stored in a three dimensional array. An example of data that can be divided into blocks is terrain: It is irregular, can't be described with a simple mathematical formula...but different cultural scapes can define the "liquid".

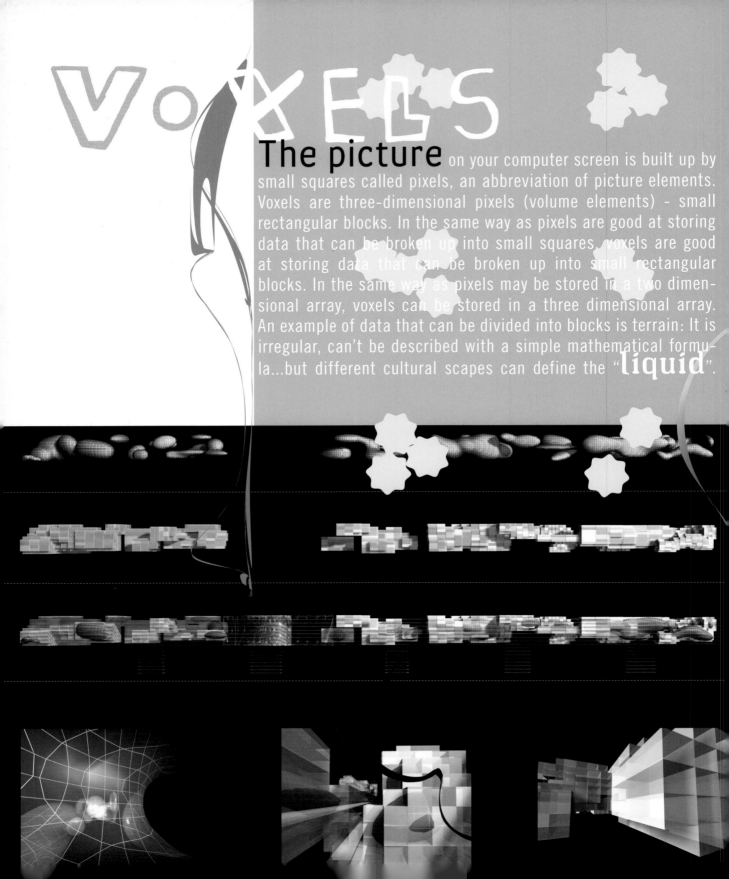

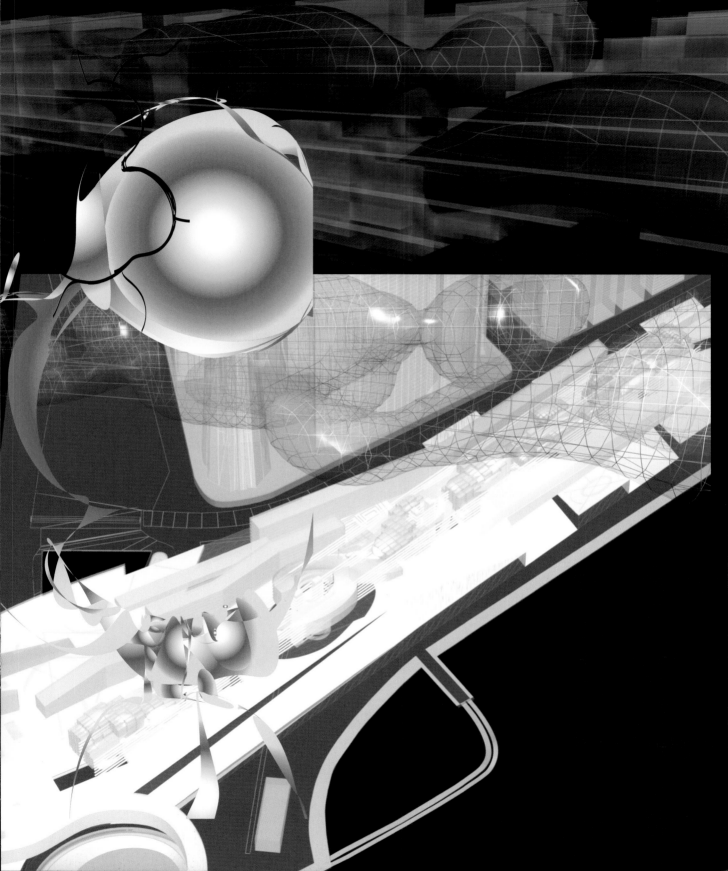

JAPAN
V=77800m³, H=39m, A=9974m² on 5levels

INDIA
V=5439m³, H=22m, A=1531m²

SOUTHAFRICA
V=3600m, H=34m, A=953m², on 9levels

BRASILIA
V=28000m³, H=34m, A=7412m², on 9levels

RUSSIA
V=30000m³, H=38m, A=7895m², on 10levels

ENGLAND
V=70000m³, H=36m, A=17500m², on 9levels

MACAO
V=18000m³, H=36m, A=2500m², on 5levels

FRANCE
V=20000m³, H=23m, A=5217m², on 6levels

GREECE
V=1800m³, H=465m, A=7933m², on 8levels

ITALY
V=1051m³, H=9,5m, A=221m², on 2levels

SPAIN
V=1900m³, H=15m, A=633m², on 5levels

SWITZERLAND
V=1000m³, H=11m, A=272m², on 3levels

AUSTRALIA
V=4500m³, H=13m, A=1038m², on 3levels

MEXICO
V=2800m³, H=18m, A=777m², on 5levels

CANADA
V=10000m³, H=19m. A=2105m², on 4levels

MAROCCO
V=2000m³, H=8m, A=750m², on 3levels

EGYPT
V=218m³, H=11m, A=618m², on 3levels

AUSTRIA
V=1700m³, H=11m, A=618m², on 4levels

KOREA
V=5000m³,H=20m, A=1500m²

PHILIPPINI
V=34000m³, H=30m, A=7933m²

LAOS
V=600m³, H=16m, A=750m²

NEPAL
V=1000m³, H=23m, A=260m², on 6levels

AREAS FOR THE WORLD CULTURAL CENTER
defined:V=320408m³, A=79191m², on 3-10levels

_world cultural center

hong kong is a 'LAND HUNGRY'
PLACE AND, FROM THE EARLY DAYS OF DEVELOPMENT,
HAS HAD TO RELY HEAVILY ON RECLAMATIONS TO SAT-
ISFY GROWING NEEDS FOR MORE HOUSING, COMMUNITY
USES, PORT ACTIVITIES AND OTHER ECONOMIC NEED.
INITIALLY, RECLAMATION WAS FORMED PRINCIPALLY
AROUND VICTORIA HARBOR.
WATERFRONT DEVELOPMENT IN HONG KONG HAS A
LONG HISTORY. IN 1981, IT WAS ESTIMATED THAT SOME
33 SQUARE KM OF LAND HAD BEEN ADDED TO HONG
KONG'S LAND AREA BY WATERFRONT RECLAMATIONS
SINCE 1841. THIS DID NOT TAKE INTO ACCOUNT MAJOR
LAND USE CHANGE THROUGH THE REDEVELOPMENT OF
EXISTING WATERFRONT LOCATIONS. SINCE 1854, THE
AMOUNT OF RECLAMATION IN HONG KONG IS EQUAL TO
ALL THE RECLAMATION DONE IN THE DAY FROM 1945.
FACED WITH A CONTINUED EXPANSION IN POPULATION

OVER THE NEXT 15 YEARS, GROWING EXPECTATIONS FOR BETTER AND MORE SPACIOUS LIVING AND WORKING ENVIRONMENTS AND THE DEVELOPMENT OF HONG KONG AS A REGIONAL HUB (THE NEEDS FOR MORE LAND FOR VARIOUS KINDS OF ACTIVITIES WILL CONTINUE TO GROW STEADILY IN BOTH SCALE AND DIVERSITY. IN THIS CONTEXT, THERE IS A NEED TO MOVE AHEAD IN A CONSIDERED WAY WITH THE DESIGN EVOLUTION OF POTENTIAL NEW HARBOR RECLAMATION SITES, EACH OF WHICH HAS A KEY ROLE TO PLAY IN SUPPORT OF THE DEVELOPMENT OF HONG KONG'S HUB FUNCTIONS AND ALSO TO FACILITATE THE RESTRUCTURING OF OBSOLETE PARTS OF THE METRO AREA. NOW THAT LARGE AREAS OF PROPOSED RECLAIMED LAND ARE BEGINNING TO APPEAR IN VARIOUS LOCATIONS AROUND THE HARBOR, THERE IS GROWING AWARENESS OF THE SIGNIFICANT CHANGES TAKING PLACE.

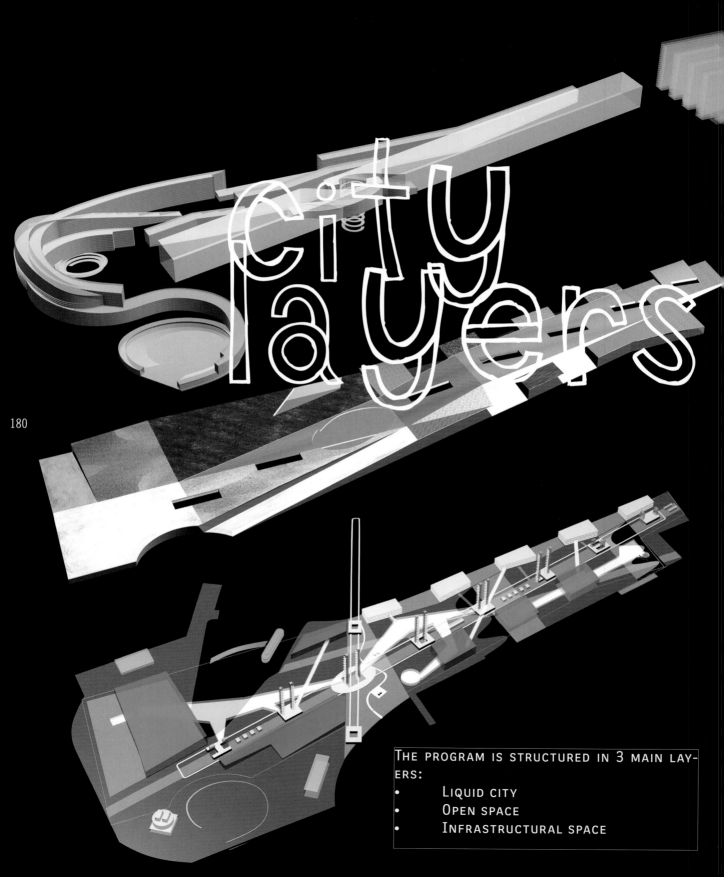

City layers

THE PROGRAM IS STRUCTURED IN 3 MAIN LAYERS:
- LIQUID CITY
- OPEN SPACE
- INFRASTRUCTURAL SPACE

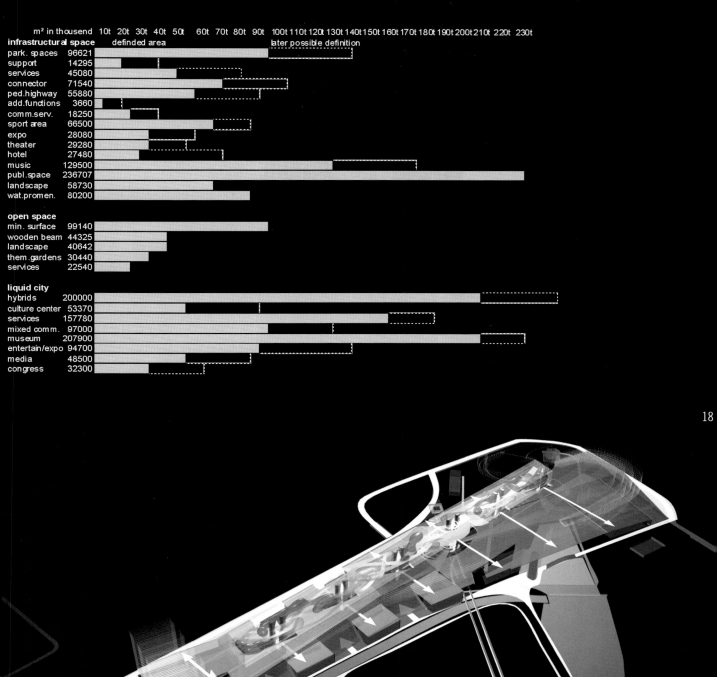

m² in thousend 10t 20t 30t 40t 50t 60t 70t 80t 90t 100t 110t 120t 130t 140t 150t 160t 170t 180t 190t 200t 210t 220t 230t

infrastructural space definded area later possible definition

park. spaces	96621
support	14295
services	45080
connector	71540
ped.highway	55880
add.functions	3660
comm.serv.	18250
sport area	66500
expo	28080
theater	29280
hotel	27480
music	129500
publ.space	236707
landscape	58730
wat.promen.	80200

open space

min. surface	99140
wooden beam	44325
landscape	40642
them.gardens	30440
services	22540

liquid city

hybrids	200000
culture center	53370
services	157780
mixed comm.	97000
museum	207900
entertain/expo	94700
media	48500
congress	32300

18

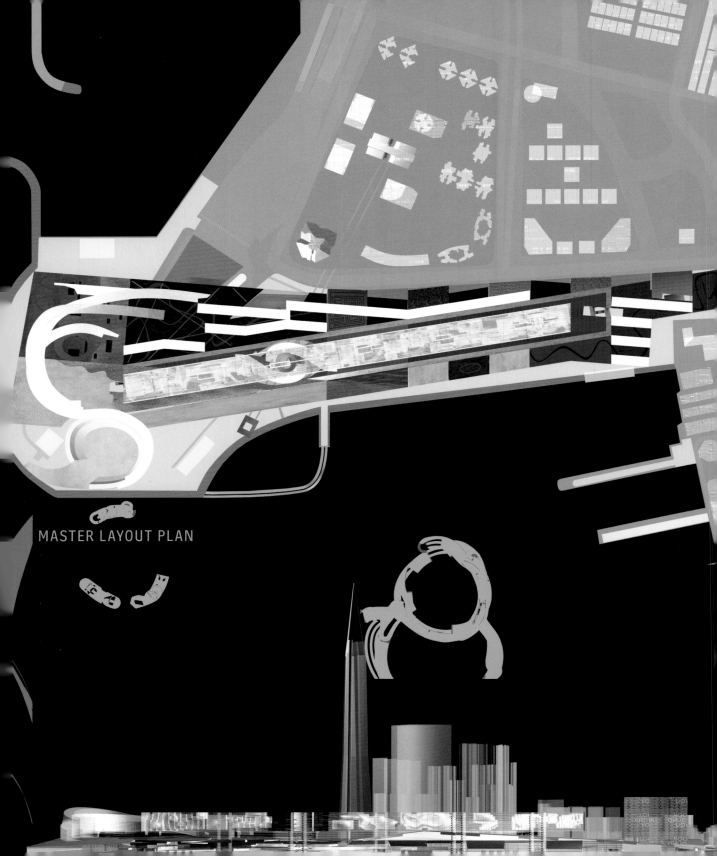

MASTER LAYOUT PLAN

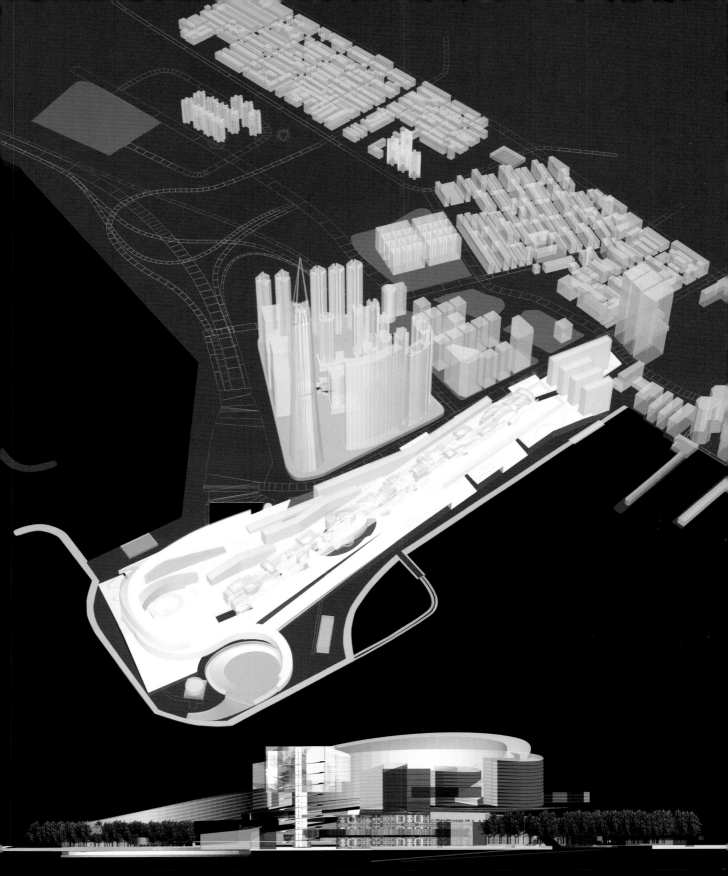

Our proposal IS BASED ON THE IDEA OF THE CITY, WHICH IS ALL OVER YOU AT THE SAME TIME: UP AND DOWN, LEFT AND RIGHT, FORWARD AND BACKWARD, WITH THE DIFFERENT QUALITY OF URBAN SEQUENCES.

THE PREVIOUSLY PLANED PARK IS SHIFTED FROM THE SITE LEVEL TO APPROXIMATELY 24 METERS IN HEIGHT. ITS BORDER

DEFINES THE BOUNDARIES OF THE INFRASTRUCTURAL LAYER (INCLUDING PARKING, VERTICAL AND HORIZONTAL TRANSPORTATION AND PEDESTRIAN WAYS AND ALL BASIC URBAN FACILITIES NECESSARY FOR ANY FUNCTIONAL CITY PART), WHICH SHOULD BE SUPPORT SPACE FOR ANY CONSTRUCTION FORM THAT THE CITY ABOVE MAY TAKE IN THE FUTURE. AS THE OUTSIDE EXTENSION OF IT THERE IS A WATERFRONT PROMENADE, WOOD AREAS, OPEN-AIR ARENA, ETC.

THE SECOND LAYER IS AN OPEN SPACE URBAN LANDSCAPE WHICH IS NOT DESIGNED IN TERMS OF ARCHITECTURAL FORMS OR BUILDINGS, BUT AS PROGRAMMED SURFACES OF DIFFERENT TEXTURES (MIN-

184

ERAL AND WOODEN MATERIALS, GRASS, THEMATIC GARDENS) BASED ON POSSIBLE LEISURE ACTIVITIES AND EVENTS. IT CAN BE FREELY ACCESSED FROM ANY LEVEL AND OCCUPIED BY CITIZENS IN UNFORESEEN WAYS.

AS AN ENDLESS STAGE, IT PROVIDES, AT THE SOUTHERN SIDE, A 1.5-KM-LONG PANORAMIC VIEW OF THE SEA AND OF THE NORTHERN SIDE OF VICTORIA HARBOUR, AND AT THE SAME TIME OPTIMIZES THE MICROCLIMATE.

THE LIQUID CITY FLOATS ABOVE THE DESCRIBED SURFACE AND IT IS A PROPOSAL FOR A POSSIBLE DEVELOPMENT OF THE BUILT-UP STRUCTURE, DENYING THE TRADITIONAL WAY OF PERCEIVING FIGURE-GROUND RELATIONSHIP. IT IS CONSIDERED AS A FROZEN "FLOW" CONDITION OF PARAMETRIC SIMULATED DESIGN PROCESS, WHICH LEAVES THE SYSTEM OPEN FOR FURTHER CHANGES AND IMPROVEMENTS. THE ONLY URBAN REGULATIONS ARE TO CONSIDER THE PROGRAM (MEDIA CENTER, ENTERTAINMENT, MUSEUMS, THEATERS, ETC.) and the woven edge condition of the over-built space, with the purpose to orientate and open the site toward south.

The additional and/or extra part is the gigantic horizontal block exactly 1-km long, which "touches" the surface only at one point. It is the WORLD CULTURAL CENTER and incorporates more then 22 nations from all over the world. This universal and global container is filled with program based on a specific culture each nation can bring to Hong Kong. The main impact of each culture is its art, music, traditional festivals, food and cooking, and all the rituals (way of life) connected to this activity, so that this element can be considered as the world's biggest kitchen of art and culture, with all supportive functions. It establishes itself not in terms of another addition to the Hong Kong skyline, but defines a new symbolic and iconographic horizon (landmark) and future perspectives.

station VI

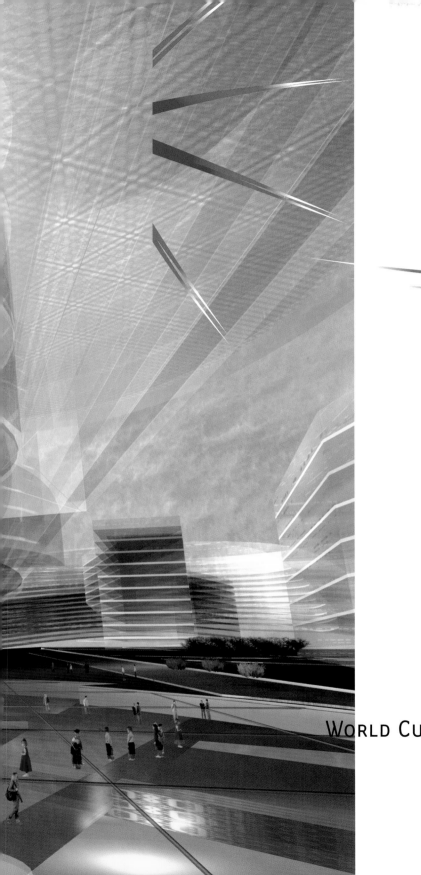

WORLD CULTURAL CENTER

MAIN SPIRAL

Teleworking House

Kotor, Montenegro

A house for a data dandy

On holiday you have two choices: either you take photos of your family in front of old buildings (look, there are the children, wife and mother-in-law at St. Tripun Cathedral), or you take photos of deserted buildings in order to consider at home how the old town can be rebuilt or what one could possibly do with this old structure — it is sooo old.

How can it be different in the case of Kotor? Kotor is very old, founded perhaps 168 B.C. The city gained its importance through the favorable

existing walls

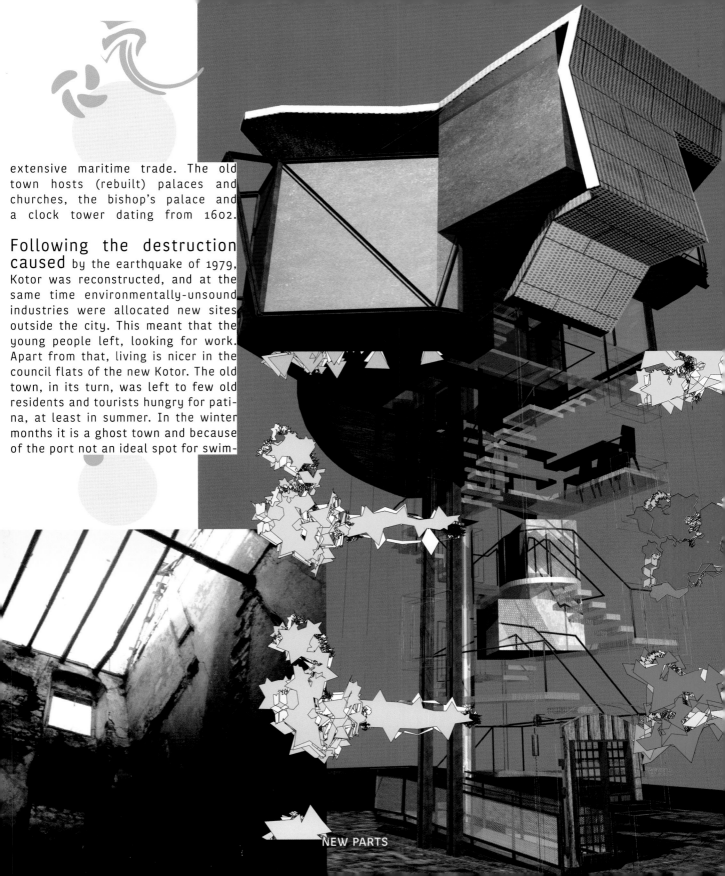

extensive maritime trade. The old town hosts (rebuilt) palaces and churches, the bishop's palace and a clock tower dating from 1602.

Following the destruction caused by the earthquake of 1979,

Kotor was reconstructed, and at the same time environmentally-unsound industries were allocated new sites outside the city. This meant that the young people left, looking for work. Apart from that, living is nicer in the council flats of the new Kotor. The old town, in its turn, was left to few old residents and tourists hungry for patina, at least in summer. In the winter months it is a ghost town and because of the port not an ideal spot for swim

NEW PARTS

ming either. No major income. The typical fate of many a town on the Adriatic coast. Has anybody got any use for this pile of building rubble? Can architecture **help?**

The conception starts with the restrictive condition that everything should remain unchanged. The new respects

the past, using it as an argument. The old town must market itself. The town-planning solution is based on the investment of private investors who are ready to put their money into individual houses. Parallel to the increasing capital, the infrastructure is being improved and what the old town has to offer is being expanded. But attractions cost a lot of money, especially because here, planning for the public is out of place. First, this makes me think of certain clients, then a data dandy. Our

friend will have a cool "home" - **dematerialized** electronic contents - that will enable him to live hundreds of miles from places to which he only has a virtual business or private relationship but, he is right by the sea, with good air, sunshine and

function

entrance

a yacht by the front door. The quality of his home is not determined by calculating the usable space, but is seen as a backdrop for events to happen, with the rooms that support this function.

The house is situated in the middle of the old town, and it is as big/small as the plot of land itself. On three sides enclosed by narrow lanes, on the fourth it borders the adjacent building. The entrance is at the eastern side opposite a chapel. The ground surface of the building is only 4.5 x 6.5 meters while its height is 9.5 meters. The tower-like construction is hollow inside, burnt out, with only the four stone walls left. A container. The old house is turned into a vase, the new is the flower put inside. 10 meters high only the stairs and ramps that define the space. It is a semi-public area, the city is led in, it is continued. The kitchen is at a height of 7 meters while all other rooms rise high above the house, like leaves. Thus, the old struc-

cockpit

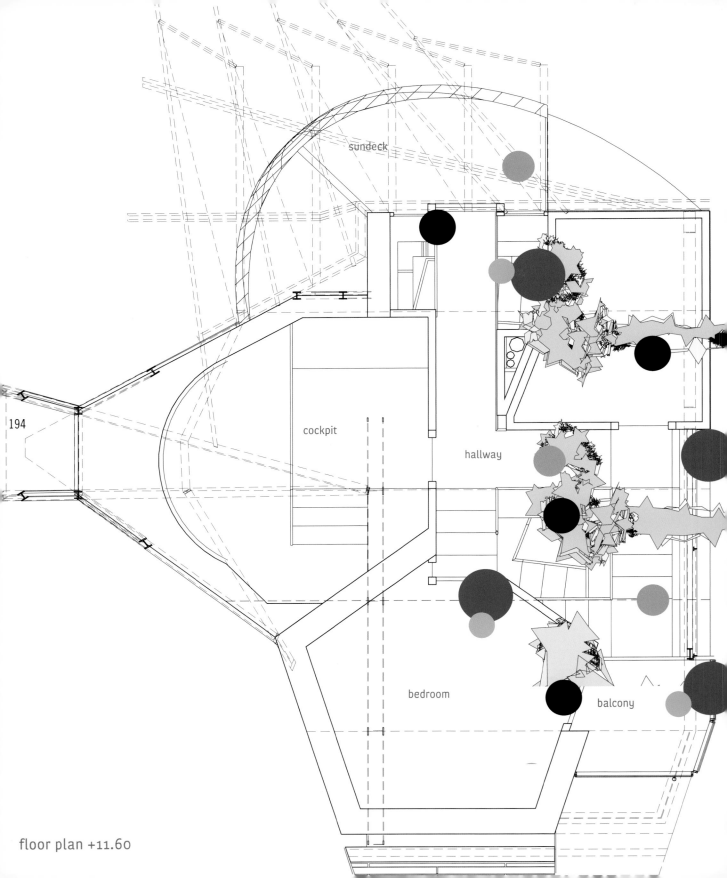

sundeck

194

cockpit

hallway

bedroom

balcony

floor plan +11.60

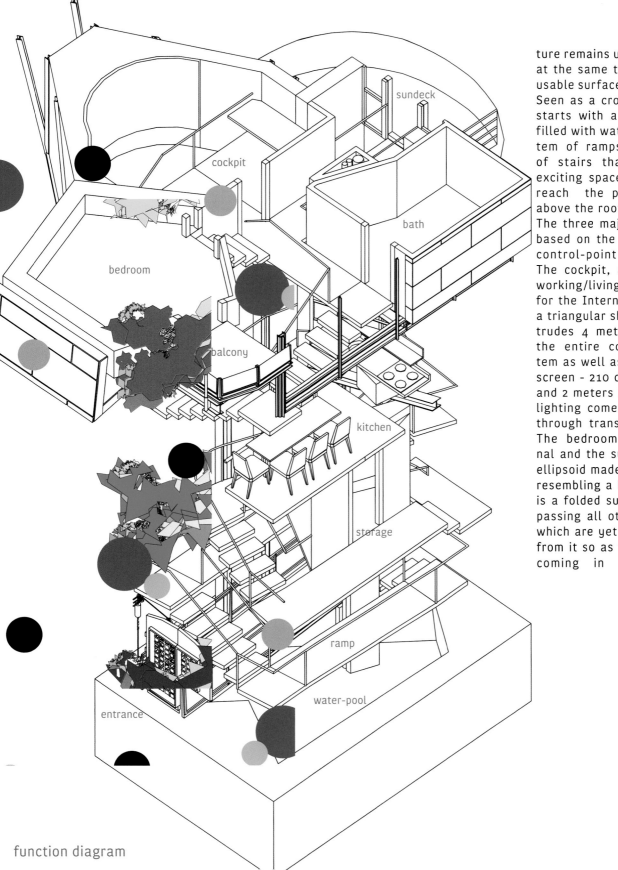

ture remains untouched and at the same time the basic usable surface is increased. Seen as a cross section, it starts with a sunken area filled with water. Via a system of ramps and flights of stairs that define an exciting space, you finally reach the program level above the roofs of the city. The three major rooms are based on the "3, 4 and 5 control-point geometry". The cockpit, a windowless working/living room, suited for the Internet cowboy, is a triangular shape and protrudes 4 meters. It hosts the entire computer system as well as a projection screen - 210 degrees round and 2 meters high. Indirect lighting comes from above through translucent glass. The bedroom is pentagonal and the sun terrace an ellipsoid made of wood and resembling a hull. The roof is a folded surface encompassing all other elements which are yet disconnected from it so as to allow light coming in **SIDEWISE**.

sundeck

cockpit

bath

bedroom

balcony

kitchen

storage

ramp

water-pool

entrance

function diagram

movie sequences

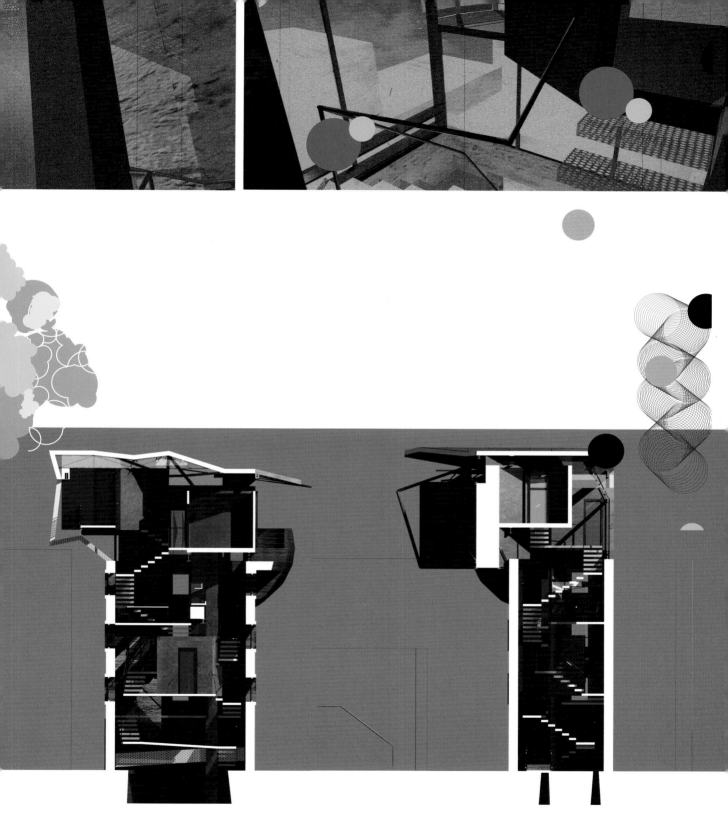

sections

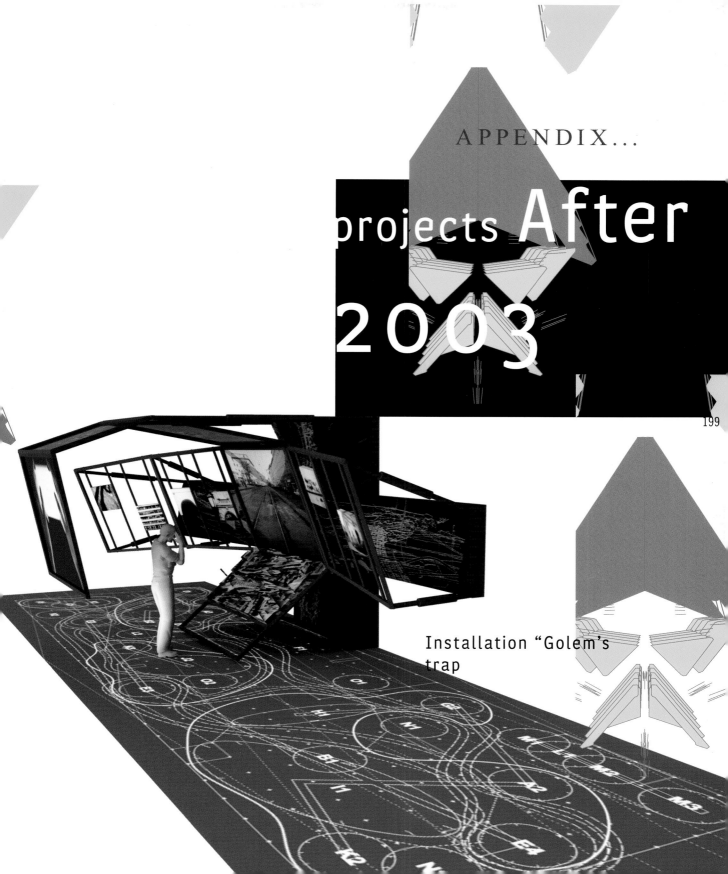

projects **After**

2003

Installation "Golem's trap

Fitnesscenter

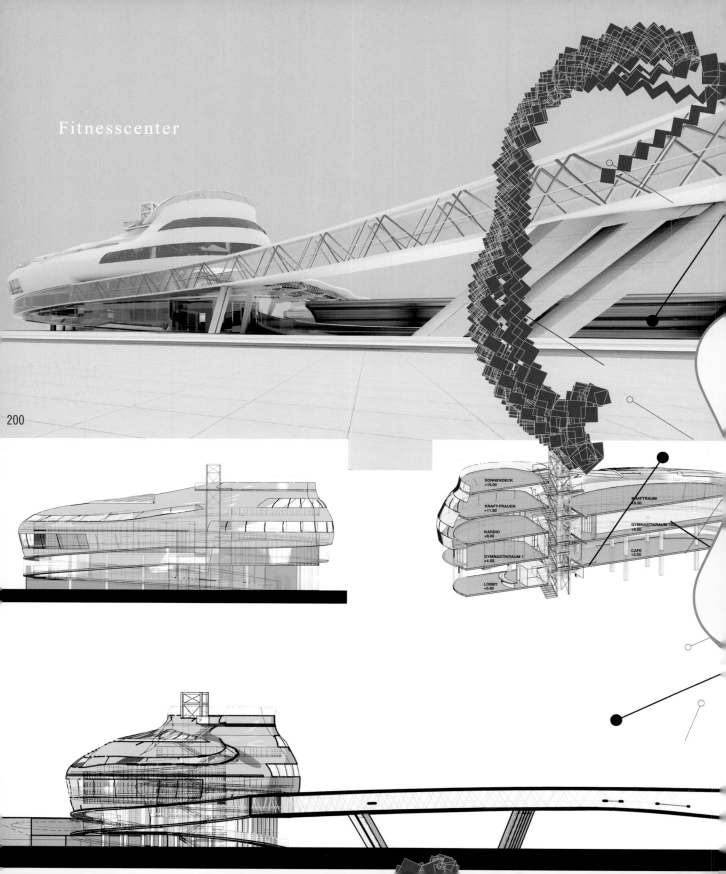

SONNENDECK
+15.00

KRAFT-FRAUEN
+11.30

KARDIO
+8.00

GYMNASTIKRAUM 1
+4.50

LOBBY
+0.80

KRAFTRAUM
+9.50

GYMNASTIKRAUM
+6.00

CAFE
+2.50

Hotel

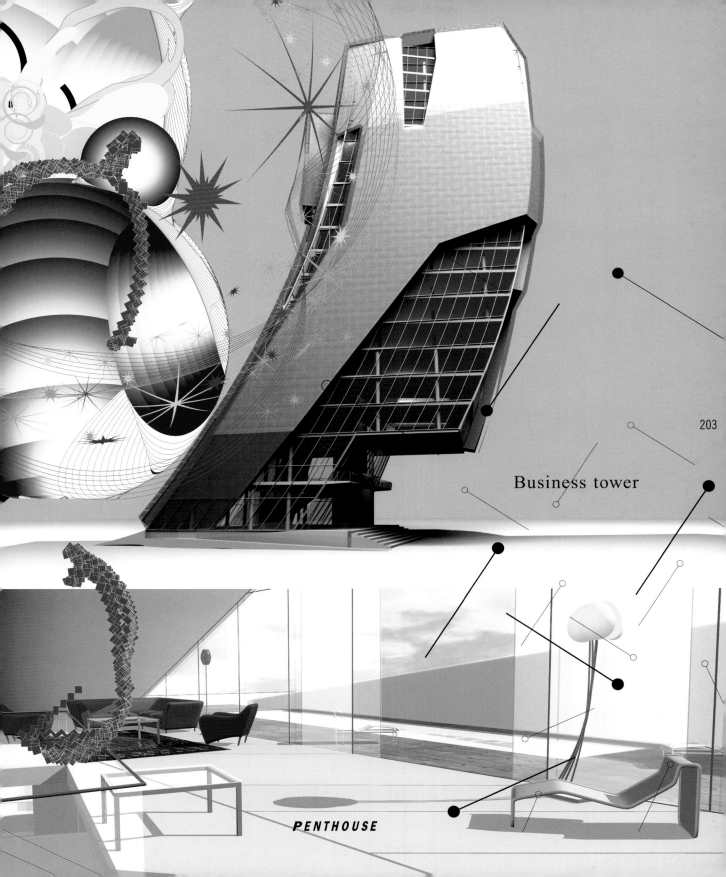

Business tower

PENTHOUSE

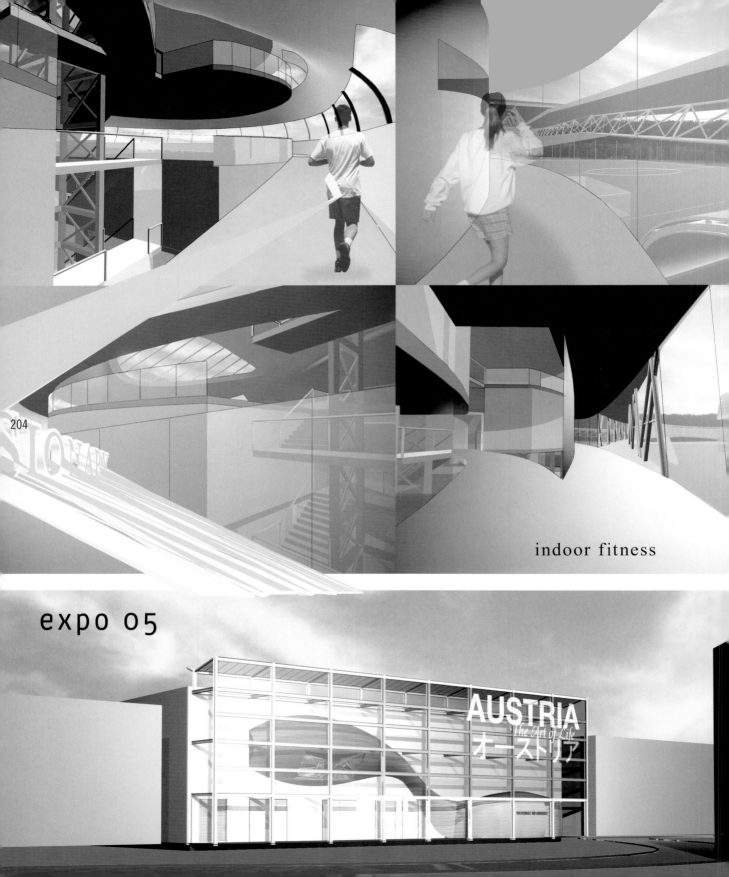

indoor fitness

expo 05

AUSTRIA
The Art of Life
オーストリア

LivingOffices

Office Building >

Motor Sports School.

Mangold Restaurant

207

XXX

Hunting
X X X museum

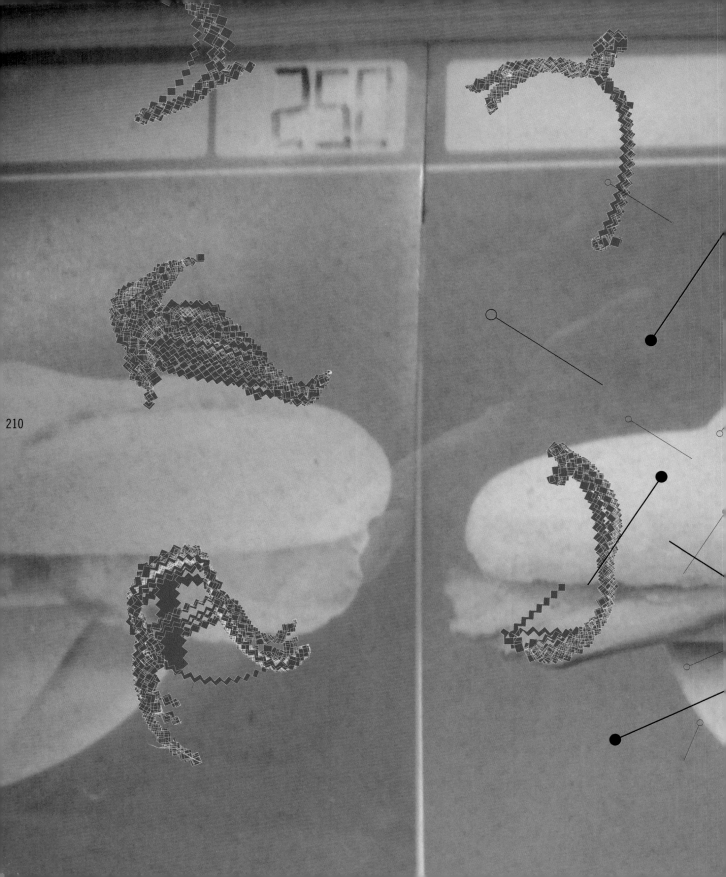

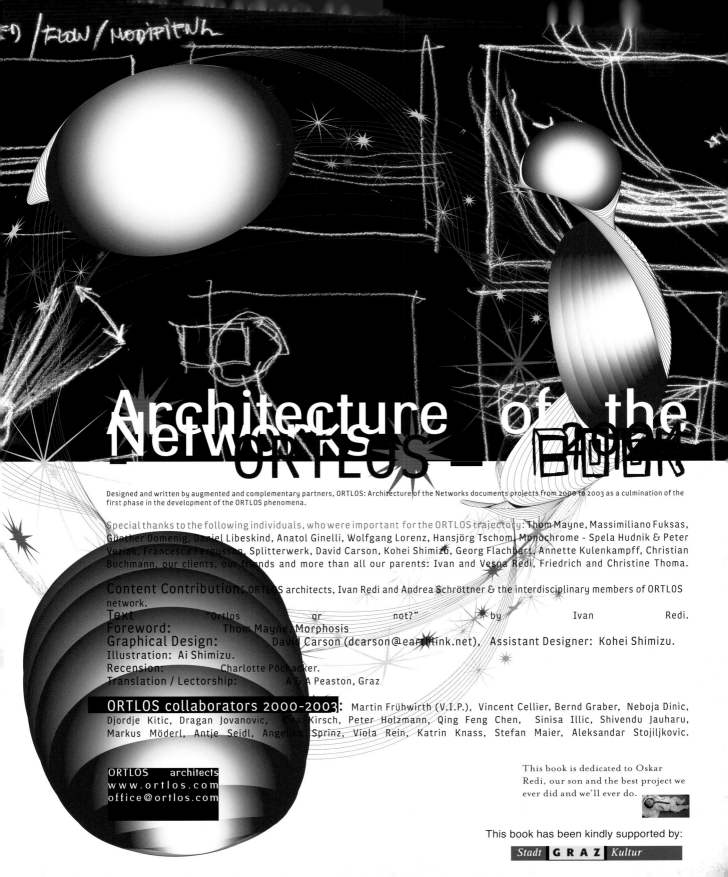

Architecture of the Networks — ORTLOS BOOK

Designed and written by augmented and complementary partners, ORTLOS: Architecture of the Networks documents projects from 2000 to 2003 as a culmination of the first phase in the development of the ORTLOS phenomena.

Special thanks to the following individuals, who were important for the ORTLOS trajectory: Thom Mayne, Massimiliano Fuksas, Günther Domenig, Daniel Libeskind, Anatol Ginelli, Wolfgang Lorenz, Hansjörg Tschom, Monochrome - Spela Hudnik & Peter Veziak, Francesca Fergusson, Splitterwerk, David Carson, Kohei Shimizu, Georg Flachbart, Annette Kulenkampff, Christian Buchmann, our clients, our friends and more than all our parents: Ivan and Vesna Redi, Friedrich and Christine Thoma.

Content Contribution: ORTLOS architects, Ivan Redi and Andrea Schröttner & the interdisciplinary members of ORTLOS network.

Text "Ortlos or not?" by Ivan Redi.

Foreword: Thom Mayne, Morphosis

Graphical Design: David Carson (dcarson@earthlink.net), Assistant Designer: Kohei Shimizu.

Illustration: Ai Shimizu.

Recension: Charlotte Pöchacker.

Translation / Lectorship: A & A Peaston, Graz

ORTLOS collaborators 2000-2003: Martin Frühwirth (V.I.P.), Vincent Cellier, Bernd Graber, Neboja Dinic, Djordje Kitic, Dragan Jovanovic, Kira Kirsch, Peter Holzmann, Qing Feng Chen, Sinisa Illic, Shivendu Jauharu, Markus Möderl, Antje Seidl, Angelika Sprinz, Viola Rein, Katrin Knass, Stefan Maier, Aleksandar Stojiljkovic.

ORTLOS architects
www.ortlos.com
office@ortlos.com

This book is dedicated to Oskar Redi, our son and the best project we ever did and we'll ever do.

This book has been kindly supported by:

Stadt GRAZ Kultur

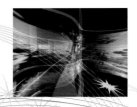

City at once - Los Angeles ____ 2000
+ 3D Computer Animations @ La Biennale in Venice

"The 16. June 2004 was quite a usual day, and nevertheless it has went into the history of the world architecture. On this day from eight o'clock until three o'clock in the morning experiences Tula Ferrera the city Los Angeles, and the observer gets to know her actions, meetings and thoughts. "City at once - Playa Vista" the city of the century: a modern adventure without comparation."

ORTLOS architects: Ivan Redi with Andrea Schröttner, Martin Frühwirth

Library for the Information Age ____ 2000
+ 3D Computer Animations @ La Biennale in Venice

This project is about a contextless, imaginative and flexible system which describes the narrative space as dualism between the space of reading and the reading of space.... the thus occurring cybrid condition does not generate space but a cybrid space can be generated through certain overlaid logics.

ORTLOS architects: Ivan Redi and Martin Frühwirth, with Andrea Schröttner

Ortlos @ La Biennale ____ 2000 Exhibition of the 7th La Biennale Venice

The concept of the installation for the theme "Less Aesthetics More Ethics", is a symbol manifesto addressing new methods of operation in architecture. It is a form tube- construction covered with a projection foil which shapes the new frame and defines the space in the space.

Client: La Biennale di Venezia 2000, Dir.Massimiliano Fuksas
ORTLOS architects: Ivan Redi, Andrea Schröttner, Martin Frühwirth, Dave Grant
Steel construction: Metallbau Treiber, Graz. Static engineer: Mitter Mang, D. Membrane structure: Trevision. Glas structure: Laserplast, Vienna. Assembly: Mit Loidl od CO. KEG Graz.
Supported by: Republic Austria, KUNST.Bundeskanzleramt; Land Steiermark, Wirtschaftspolitik & Telekommunikation und Büro des Landeshauptmann Stv. der Stmk. ;
Stadt Graz Kulturamt, Stadtentwicklung, Stadtbaudirektion; Metallbau Treiber Graz, Interunfall Graz, Trevision und Laserplast Wien, Mitter Mang, D; mit LOIDL od CO KEG, Graz; ACP Austria & Compaq computers, Salzburg; Repro Bauer, Graz; Paul Ott, Photograph, Graz; Spedition Jöbstl KG, Graz

inSPACEin ____ 2001
Study, Mobile Information - Communication Environment

We create an architecturally formulated information-communication environment filled with the cultural content based on the program for Graz, cultural capital of Europe 2003. As a first thought, we define an area in the area. The superimpostion of parallel realities and media should occur. "Moving Walls", "Video Floor", image projections, "broken information strips" are elements that should form this area and shape it unpredictably and constantly through change. So, the space shifts from "moving bodies through space" into "moving space with bodies".

Client: Graz Cultural Capital 2003, Wolfgang Lorenz
ORTLOS architects: Ivan Redi and Andrea Schröttner with Martin Frühwirth, Djorde Kitic, Bernd Graber, Viola Rein

212

A.N.D.I. - A New Digital Instrument ____ for networked creative collaboration 2001 - 2004
Research project

A.N.D.I. will provide a virtual office structure in the Internet where its users can work together independent of their location, for the conception, design and production of architectural and art projects. This digital platform is an operating system, a tool to work at an interdisciplinary and international level during each project but in particular from the very beginning of the design to increase the project's creative dimension.

Client: "Open source project"
ORTLOS architects: Ivan Redi and Andrea Schröttner with Vincent Cellier, Martin Frühwirth, Kira Kirsch, Peter Holzmann
Programmer: Neboja Dinic, Dragan Jovanovic. Project Management: Ferenc Schröttner. ORTLOS network: Martin Krusche, Net.Literat; Maja Engeli & Kerstin Hoegger, Research Architects
Supported by: Republic Austria, KUNST.Bundeskanzleramt; Stadt Graz. Kulturamt; Land Steiermark, Abteilung Kunst & Abteilung für Wissenschaft und Forschung; Kultur Kontakt - Austria

THE GRAND EGYPTIAN MUSEUM ____ 2002 Competition , Giza Egypt

The main idea is to make a light, open and floating structure, - as opposed to the monolithic building type and closed singular static shapes - with an internal organizational network, which supports our museum's concept: the Network of Experience and Knowledge. The new museum is not a unitary totality, but a heterotopia. The image of our project is based on the tension between fluidity vs. materiality, dynamic vs static, open vs. closed. There is no up or down. The building like a city - completely surrounds us: the virtual structures of the museum are connected to each other at every conceivable angle; there is no horizon either; the mesh of building-like shapes stretches in all directions.

Client: Ministry of Culture - Supreme Council of Antiquities (SCA)- Arab Republic of Egypt
ORTLOS architects: Ivan Redi and Andrea Schröttner with Qing Feng Chen, Peter Holzman, Shivendu Jauhari

Graz 2003 -
Cultural Capital of Europe

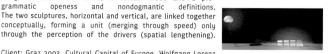

"The Thing and The Wing" symbolizes a state of mobility, distortion and flows, a certain mood and a programmatic openess and nondogmantic definitions. The two sculptures, horizontal and vertical, are linked together conceptually, forming a unit (merging through speed) only through the perception of the drivers (spatial lengthening).

Client: Graz 2003, Cultural Capital of Europe, Wolfgang Lorenz ORTLOS architects: Ivan Redi, Andrea Schröttner and Martin Frühwirth with Bernd Graber, Viola Rein. Light: Erich Stifter, LG - Elektrotechnik Licht. Static construction: Zenkner & Handel, Fazheli & Wolfesberger. Metall construction: Heidenbauer Metallbau, SFL Metallbau. Concret construction: Wilfling Hoch und Tiefbau. Fiber-Glas construction: Kucharz, artist. Projection Membrane: Typico. Fotos: Angelo Kaunat, Paul Ott, ORTLOS architects. Supported by: Heiden-

bauer Metallbau, Wilfling Hoch und Tiefbau, LG-Elektrotechnik Licht.

The Thing & The Wing Songs ____ 2003
ORTLOS music with Vik

Music production for an architectural project. "The Thing & The Wing can be everything, the Thing & The Wing can mean anything" is the refrain of the song, especially written and produced for this project, which should intensify the aspect of the dynamic, movement and speed.
Idea, conception & production: ORTLOS architects, Ivan Redi and Andrea Schröttner. Text & Music: Ivan Redi. Lead singer: Viktor Beck. Remixes: Nomix, Herwig Baumgartner, Nevenko Bucan, Roland Lindner. Cover graphic design: Tomislav Bobinec. Images: ORTLOS architects. Sound Mastering: Nomix Supported by Graz 2003 cultural capital of Europe.

KUNSTHAUS ____ 2000
Competition, Graz, Austria

Our proposal can be divided into two essential concepts. The first one expands urban space on the ground floor level, acting as an attractor for the surrounding squares, lanes, and street systems by beeing accessible and permeable, and thus even the most public sphere runs directly into the radius of the Kunsthaus.
The second proposal expands the concept of exhibition room as such by an Identity-generating shell whose potentialities are nourished by expanding work/author/spectator-aided concepts of contemporary art therefore define two integrative approaches that are enabled and translated through architecture.

Client: Die Stadt Graz, Austria
ORTLOS architects: Ivan Redi and Andrea Schröttner with Quing Feng Chen, Peter Holzman, Djordje Kitic.
Project Partners: Andreas Lechner, Matthias Bauer

213

lighThing ____ 2003
Interior design, LighThing

The lighThing is modeled based on "The Thing" the vertical element of the "The Thing & The Wing" installation. The lighThing is an artistic light sculpture for the interior and is produced as limited edition. The lighThing transforms the room with it's different light settings.

ORTLOS architects: Ivan Redi and Andrea Schröttner with Markus Möderl, Antje Seidl, Bernd Graber, Peter Holzmann.
Partner for Prototype: Erich Stifter & LG-Elektrotechnik Licht. Metal construction: Eduard Dorner. Light /technic: LG-Elektrotechnik Licht. Polymer object: Kessler Kunststoffverarbeitung. Concrete part: Prenner GesmbH. Color photographs: Angelo Kaunat / www.kaunat. com. B/W: Ivan Redi

URBAN PARK ____ 2001
Competition, Central Urban Park, La Paz, Bolivia

The design intention follows the topographic gestures of the landscape with a geometric system of generated layers to make use of the panorama qualities and the levels of the site: the green grove of La Paz will consist of a complex system of terraced wedges, a portfolio of landscape elements that suggest recreation potentials in groups as well as in peaceful isolation.
The "poetic layer" is developed by the Artist Günther Brus, he create 12 sentences for the project a sort of "poetic pattern" which are the main connectors or inspirations for the formal expressions. They build the sequences of sections for the open story of the park.

Client: Municipal Government of La Paz, Bolivien
ORTLOS architects: Ivan Redi and Andrea Schröttner with Martin Frühwirth, Vincent Cellier
Projectpartner: Artist Günther Brus. Landscape architects: Auböck & Karas - Vienna. Translations: Sarah Steiner, Eva Ferraz.

Teleworking House ____ 1998
A house for a data dandy, Kotor, Montenegro

The conception starts with the restrictive condition that everything should remain unchanged. The new respects the past, using it as an argument. The old town must market itself.
The old house is turned into a vase, the new is the flower put inside. 10 meters high only the stairs and ramps that define the space. It is a semi-public area, the city is led in, it is continued. The kitchen is at a height of 7 meters while all other rooms rise high above the house, like leaves.
Thus the old structure remains untouched and at the same time the basic usable surface is increased.
The three major rooms are based on the "3, 4 and 5 control-point geometry". The cockpit, a windowless working/living room, suited for the Internet cowboy, is a triangular shape and hosts the entire computer system as well as a projection screen - 210 degrees round and 2 meters high.

Architect: Ivan Redi

West Kowloon Reclamation ____ 2001
Competition, Hong Kong

Our proposal is based on the idea of the city, which is all over you at the same time: up and down, left and right, forward and backward, with the different quality of urban sequences. The program is structured in 3 main layers: Infrastructural space, Open space, Liquid city. The liquid city floats above the described surface and it is a proposal for a possible development of the built up structure, denying the traditional way of perceiving figure-ground relationship. It is considered as a frozen "flow" condititon of parametric simulated design process, which leaves the system open for further changes and improvements. The additional extra part is the gigantic horizontal block exactly 1km long, which "touches" the surface only at one point. It is the "World Cultural Center" and incorporates more then 22 nations from all over the world.

Client: Government of Hong Kong, China
ORTLOS architects: Ivan Redi and Andrea Schröttner with Martin Frühwirth, Vincent Cellier

Selected Projects

2005:

• Jagdkundemuseum Schloss Stainz - competition, Stainz, Austria
• Haus des Verkehrs - competition, Graz, Austria

2004:

• Haus Augustin/Schebesta, single family house, Graz Austria
• Businesstower, including offices, restaurants,.. Graz, Austria
• Austrian Pavilion Expo 2005, Japan – competition (2nd round), Vienna, Austria
• Hart, community center – invited competition, Hart bei Graz, Austria

2003:

• A.N.D.I. [A New Digital Instrument for networked creative collaboration], research project, Graz, Austria, 2001-2003
• Schwechat, housing estate – competition, Vienna, Austria
• "The Thing & The Wing", Project for Graz 03, Cultural Capital of Europe, Graz, Austria
• Haus Renner, one family house, Graz, Austria

2002:

• inSPACEin, project study, Graz, Austria
• Rinnergründe, procedure for calling in expert opinion, Gratkorn, Austria
• Grand Egyptian Museum - competition, Giza, Egypt

2001:

• Mangolds Restaurant, Re-build, Graz, Austria
• West Kowloon Reclamation – competition, Hong Kong, China
• La Paz Urban Park – competition, La Paz, Bolivia

2000:

• Venice Biennale of Architecture, exhibition & installation, Venice, Italy
• The Library for the Information Age: space of reading/reading of space – competition, ACADIA, Pittsburgh, USA
• City at once. Playa Vista. Los Angeles, project study, Graz Austria

Selected Publications

2004

Camp for Oppositional Architecture (Berlin, June 04) AN Architektur "A.N.D.I.- A New Digital Instrument for Networked creative collaboration - a research project" p. 96-97

Architektur & Bau Forum (20), 12.11.2004, "Open Source Architecture" p.6

2003

CONCEPT- Architecture & Concept
Nr. 05, 2003, Seoul/ Korea, p. 46-55.
"ORTLOS architects – The Thing & The Wing"

ARCHITEKTUR.AKTUELL
Nr. 06, 2003, June/July, p. 121-136
„Graz 2003 – Städtebau als Kommunikations-Kunst"

KUNSTHAUS GRAZ, Documentation of the competition
HDA (edit.)
Haus der Architektur, 2003, Graz, Austria, p. 112
„ORTLOS Architekten"

2002

Arch+Ing – KONSTRUKTIV
Nr. 233, Sept./ Oct. 2002, Vienna/ Austria, p. 18-19
"Planen und Bauen mit Computern"

CA – Contemporary Architecture
Nr. 42, 2002-3, Seoul/ Korea, p. 128-139
"ORTLOS ARCHITECTS – Association for Experimental Architecture and Interface"

AMBIENT
Nr. 44, December 2002, Lubiljana/ Slovenija, p. 109-114
"Gradec – kava in kultura"

UNSCHAERFERELATIONEN Experiment Raum
Karin Damrau, Anton Markus Pasing (edit.):
H.M. Nelte Publishing, 2002, Wiesbaden, Germany, p. 113-115
"ORTLOS – A.N.D.I."

2001

PARPAINGS
No. 20, 02/01, Paris, France, p. 16-19
„Expressions →Ortlos Architects"

AB, architect´s bulletin
No. 153-154, 11/01, p. 46-51
„Ortlos Life-Style"

THE ARCHITECTURE OF INTELLIGENCE
Derrick de Kerckhove
Birkhaeuser Publishing, 2001, Basel, Switzerland, p. 70-71
"Principles of Connected Architecture"

NCC48
Netart Community Congress, october 2001, Internet
„open source/free software", „net-art"

2000

ARCHITEKTUR AKTUELL
No. 243/244, July/Aug. 2000, Vienna, Austria, p. 94-101
"Architektur als Symbol"

ARCHITEKTUR & BAU FORUM
No. 208, Sept./Oct. 2000, Vienna, Austria, p. 75-81
„ortlos: space off - ortlos at la biennale"

ARCHITEKTUR AKTUELL
No. 245, Sep. 2000, Vienna, Austria, p. 108 – 115, p. 57
"Vom Masterplan zum Stadt-Drehbuch", „to be ortlos"

PASAJES DE ARQUITECTURA Y CRITICA
No. 19, Sep. 2000, Madrid, Spain, p. 50
"Ortlos. Arquitectura conectiva"

ZOO
Nov. 2000, London, GB, p. 84 – 85
"Venice Biennale - Feature - ortlos architects"

PROFIL
No. 25, 06/19/00, p. 178
"Ortlos in Venedig"

Lectures/ Presentations/ Exhibitions

2005

City Upgrade - High Spirited Networked City, steirisc[:her:]bst 2005, 30.09-30.10.2005

2004

OS04 - Event "OpenSource and architecture", Lecture, 22/10/04, Graz, Austria, "A.N.D.I.-Open Source and Architecture"

Open Source Architecture - city upgrade, lecture 15/11/04, Graz, Austria, "architecture of the networks"

Architekturtage 2004, 4+5. June, movie presentation "the mak-

ing of the Thing & the Wing"

Open Source Architecture - City Upgrade, Forum Stadtpark, 15.11-19.11.2004

Expo 2005 Aichi, Japan, presentation for the Austrian Pavilion
EXPO 2005, 22.10-19.12.2004, HDA (House of Architects) Graz, Austria

6. Internationaler medien und architektur Preis, Think tank "Architektur & Medien Biennale" - Kunsthaus Graz

2003

PUNKT 7 – 30 minutes architecture from Graz
Lecture, 03/13/03, Graz, Austria
"The Thing & The Wing"

NCC03 - net.art community congress
Presentation, 10/24/03, Graz, Austria
„A.N.D.I. [A New Digital Instrument]"

Seventh Belgrade Triennal of World Architecture
Exhibition, 06/27 – 08/09/03, Belgrade, Serbia
„Global Dream: ORTLOS architects"

Technical University Vienna
Lecture, 06/18/03, Vienna, Austria
"net.work.space"

Art pavilion „Cvijeta Zuzoric"
Exhibition, 08/09/03, Belgrade, Serbia
"beyond the light"

2002

FRISCHE FISCHE aus dem Architektenpool
Exhibition, October 2002, Graz, Austria
"Exhibition on Tour: Wien, Oslo, Feldkirch, Budapest, Graz"

2001

OeGFA (Austrian Society for Architecture)
Lecture, 01/19/01, Haus Wittgenstein, Vienna, Austria
"ortlos on_line"

hdax
Lecture, 11/02/01, Haus der Architektur, Graz, Austria
"unsere Zeit ist gekommen!...aber gleich wieder vergangen."

NCC 48, Netart Community Congress
Congress, 10/25-10/27/01, Graz Austria
„A.N.D.I. [A New Digital Instrument]"

2000

7th Venice Biennale of Architecture
Exhibition 06/18 – 10/29/00 Venice, Italy
"Less Aesthetics more Ethics"

KIG! Jubiläum Presentation, 04/26 -04/28/01, Graz, Austria
"Citta: Less Aesthetic More Ethics, The Library for the Information Age,City at once, Playa Vista, LA"
Millenium Performance
Performance, 12/31/00 – 01/01/01,Graz, Austria "millenium@ortlos/night-performance.mp3 deconstruction"

9th Salon for Urbanism
Exhibition 11/00, Nis, Serbia
„City at Once"

berlinbeta
Lecture 08/30 – 09/06/00 Berlin, Germany
"We no longer have roots, we have aerials"

Bionic Territories , International Festival "Architecture and New Media"
Video-Installation , 10/19/- 10/22/00, Ljubljana, Slovenia
"The Library for the Information Age: space of reading/ reading of space".

Various awards for the excellent web design.

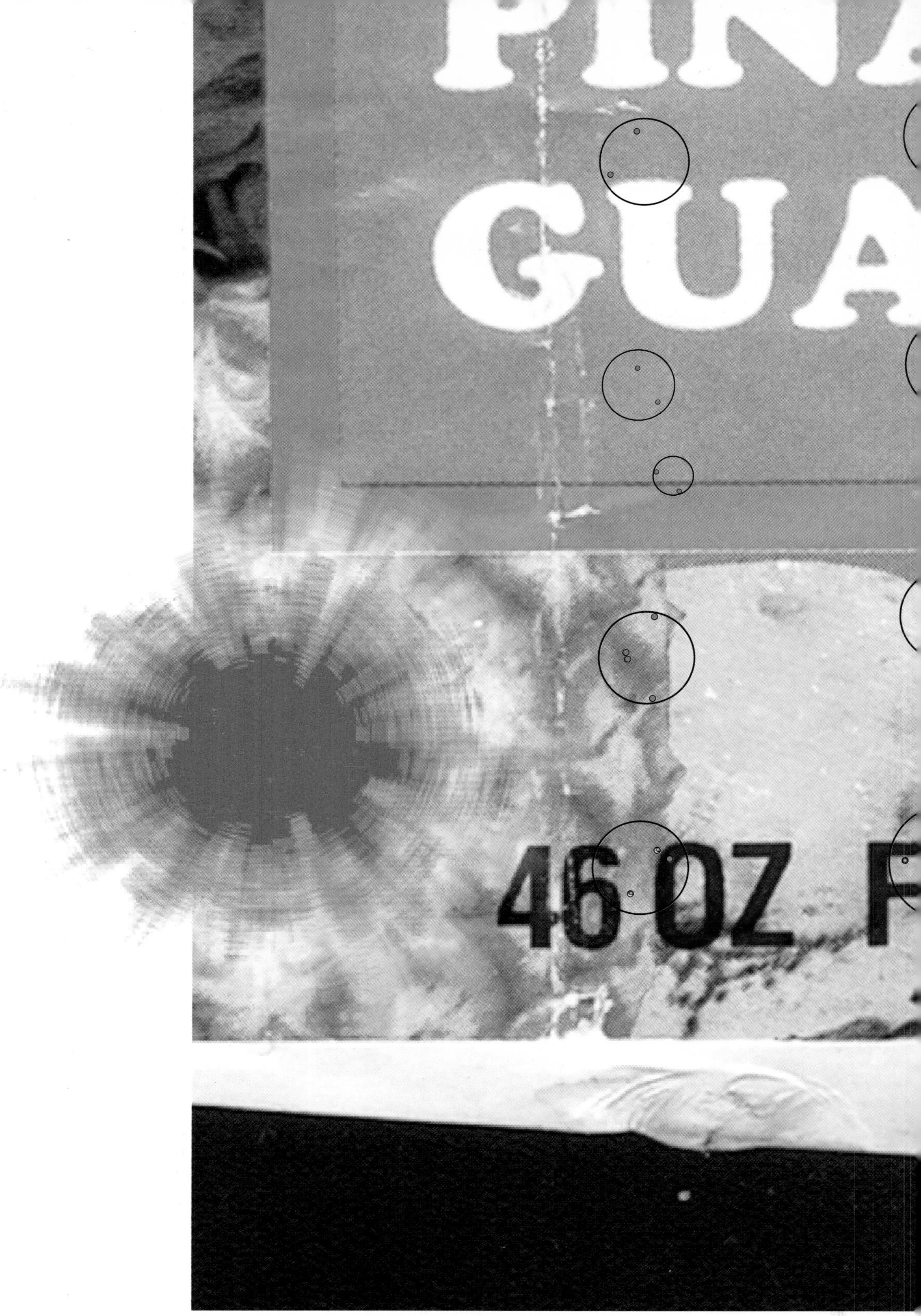
46 OZ